100

THINGS TO DO IN
NASHVILLE
BEFORE YOU
DIE

2nd Edition

D1502723

Enjoy the Omni's Nashville!

— Tom Adkinson

2nd Edition

100
THINGS TO DO IN
NASHVILLE
BEFORE YOU
DIE

• •

TOM ADKINSON

REEDY PRESS

Library of Congress Control Number: 2018945634

ISBN: 9781681061665

Design by Jill Halpin

All photos by Tom Adkinson

Printed in the United States of America
18 19 20 21 22   5 4 3 2

Please note that websites, phone numbers, addresses, and company names are subject to change or cancellation. We did our best to relay the most accurate information available, but due to circumstances beyond our control, please do not hold us liable for misinformation. When exploring new destinations, please do your homework before you go.

DEDICATION

For Mike Alley, my best friend from high school,
with whom I first explored so much of Nashville.
I wish he were here to help with this book.

For the many people today who continue to explore
Nashville with me and who introduce me to Nashville
experiences and treasures I might never find on my own.

CONTENTS

● ●

Sports and Recreation

● ●

Culture and History

• •

PREFACE

Nashville has brought me joy, memorable experiences, and great surprises. I was seven when I arrived and have been here ever since—except for college in Knoxville and a few years of exile in Alabama.

As a child, I watched minor league hockey games at the Municipal Auditorium; snuck under the fence into Cheekwood; ate chili at Varallo's; prowled uninvited through the barn at Belle Meade Plantation; saw plays at Nashville Children's Theatre; poked around pawnshops on Deaderick Street (my parents didn't know); peered out from the observation deck of the L&C Tower, Nashville's first skyscraper; marveled at the huge schooners of beer my father ordered at the Gerst House; wondered why the Parthenon was such a big deal; and much more.

In other words, I had early encounters with many of Nashville's special places and activities.

As an adult, I worked for Opryland, the Grand Ole Opry, and the many components of that hydra-headed entertainment conglomerate. I knew Roy Acuff and Minnie Pearl, and they knew me. I sat in on recording sessions, helped a bit with the revival of the Ryman Auditorium, watched downtown Nashville come back from the dead, was able to buy my father a mixed drink when that finally was legal, hiked forested trails mere miles from the state Capitol, learned to navigate East Nashville's labyrinth of streets, and was a personal guide to Nashville for many visitors.

In other words, I never stopped finding Nashville's special places and activities, and I hope this book helps you have similar experiences. I extend special thanks to the many people who helped with this project. Among them:

- Lois Adkinson: Fellow explorer and great proofreader
- Jim Brown: Author, neighbor, fellow fisherman
- Pat Embry: Entertainment expert at NowPlayingNashville.com
- Mary Hance: The *Tennessean*'s "Ms. Cheap"
- Les Kerr: Purveyor of his own musical style (hillbilly blues Caribbean rock 'n' roll)
- Ellen Jones Pryor: My guide to the art world
- Lauren LeStourgeon: The eyes of youth
- Trish McGee: Knower of almost everything
- Heather Middleton: Nashville Convention & Visitors Corp. media guru
- Dan Rogers: Opry oracle
- Karen-Lee Ryan: Fellow food lover
- John Sharpe: Wise counselor
- Bob Sircy: Chauffeur and marketing counselor
- Mark Thien: Well-rooted Nashville transplant

FOOD AND DRINK

DRESS UP FOR DINNER
AT THE CAPITOL GRILLE

Sometimes you just want to dress up and savor an elegant dinner with someone you love in a restaurant that prepares memorable food and serves it with style. That's when you go to the Capitol Grille, the culinary showplace of the *Forbes Travel Guide* Five-Star Hermitage Hotel. It has been pleasing guests since 1910. The Capitol Grille understood quality and freshness of ingredients before anyone ever uttered "farm to table." Much of the restaurant's beef comes from the hotel's own sustainable cattle program, and seasonal vegetables come from an urban garden south of downtown on a Land Trust of Tennessee historic property that the hotel maintains. All this goodness comes to you in a quiet dining room where you can actually talk with your loved one.

231 Sixth Ave. N.
615-345-7116
capitolgrillenashville.com

SHAKE IT UP
ON ELLISTON PLACE

Sometimes, all you want is an honest-to-goodness milkshake. Not something artificial from a dispenser, but a real milkshake made by a real person in a soda shop—the kind with rich ice cream and perhaps an extra squirt of chocolate syrup blended in a stainless-steel container attached to a mixer that sounds like an airplane engine and leaves a circle of frost on the outside. That kind. That's when you head to the Elliston Place Soda Shop, Nashville's oldest restaurant in its original location. The fun began in 1939. It's a very respectable meat-and-three, and its pies are famous, but the milkshakes (made with Nashville's Purity ice cream) built the legend. Just ask the many fathers who have raced across the street from Saint Thomas Midtown Hospital while their wives were in labor. Sometimes, only a real milkshake will do.

2111 Elliston Pl.
615-327-1090
ellistonplacesodashop.com

ENJOY SOME VEGGIES
AT SWETT'S RESTAURANT

Meat-and-three restaurants are a hallmark of Nashville's traditional food scene. Of course, the "three" means vegetables, and these are down-home plate fillers. Meat-and-three vegetables don't crunch, and macaroni and cheese is considered one of them. Swett's Restaurant, on the cusp of North Nashville and West Nashville off Charlotte Pike, is one of the city's storied meat-and-threes. It opened in 1954 and is well into its second generation of family operation. Meats including fried chicken, ribs, meatloaf, and beef tips are complemented by a rotating array of more than a dozen vegetables—squash casserole, boiled okra, sweet potatoes, creamed corn, green beans, stewed tomatoes, and more. Count on turnip greens or collard greens every day. Swett's cooks about seven hundred pounds of greens a week. Save room for peach or blackberry cobbler.

Swett's Restaurant
2725 Clifton Ave.
615-329-4418
swettsrestaurant.com

TIP

Arnold's Country Kitchen downtown is a big-time meat-and-three favorite that has even has gotten recognition from the James Beard Foundation. You know it's good when its customers include top-flight chefs Sean Brock from Husk and Tandy Wilson from City House. For details: arnoldscountrykitchen.com

PASS THE PEAS, PLEASE,
AT MONELL'S

If you don't have friends to dine with, you can get an instant group of friends at Monell's in the Germantown neighborhood. This old house (built in 1898), with its well-worn hardwood floors and homey atmosphere, seats seventy-two people at communal tables, and bowls get passed from the left. Conversation flows around and across the tables as the fried chicken, pot roast, green beans, cheese grits, crowder peas, turnip greens, salads, and other treats move along. If a bowl or platter is emptied, a full one magically appears. Owner Michael King has dished up this all-you-want-to-eat boarding house delight since 1995. King makes a particular Southern aphorism come to life: "Enter as strangers, leave as friends."

1235 Sixth Ave. N.
615-248-4747
monellstn.com

TIP
A second location, Monell's at the Manor, is in a historic mansion near Nashville International Airport. Service is family-style here, too, and it is the setting for numerous weddings and private events.

WALK, EAT, REPEAT
ON A FOOD TOUR

Nashville's hyperactive restaurant scene, where a major new restaurant seems to open every week, is almost impossible to track. That's why food tours, such as the tasty itineraries of Walk Eat Nashville, are so useful. With routes in East Nashville, Midtown, and Downtown, Walk Eat Nashville's guides (all food writers or former journalists) provide tastes at multiple restaurants, plus background information about the city's history and culinary scene. For instance, one East Nashville tour covers about 1.5 miles in three hours and includes six tastings at establishments such as Marché Artisan Foods, Lockeland Table, and I Dream of Weenie, a most unusual hotdog emporium housed in a VW bus. Pump your guide for information about some of the city's newest places before going home for a nap.

615-587-6138
walkeatnashville.com

TIP
Nashville Originals is a consortium of more than fifty well-established, locally owned restaurants with loyal followings. They range from decidedly casual to white-tablecloth establishments. For details: nashvilleoriginals.com.

BUTTER A BISCUIT
AT THE LOVELESS CAFE

The Loveless Cafe's website offers dozens of down-home recipes, but not the top-secret one for the buttermilk biscuits that made this unassuming roadside restaurant nationally famous. Loveless biscuits first popped out of the oven in 1951 when Lon and Annie Loveless began selling fried chicken and biscuits along that era's main highway between Nashville and Memphis. Today, this spot on Highway 100 is the Natchez Trace Parkway's northern terminus. Cafe ownership changed over the decades, but not the biscuits (up to ten thousand are baked daily) or the dedication to country cooking, homemade preserves, and delicious smoked meats. Expect competition for the cafe's 129 seats. The prestigious James Beard Foundation invited the Loveless Cafe to serve Valentine's Day dinner at the James Beard House in 2013. The New York sophisticates cleaned their plates.

8400 Hwy. 100
615-646-9700
lovelesscafe.com

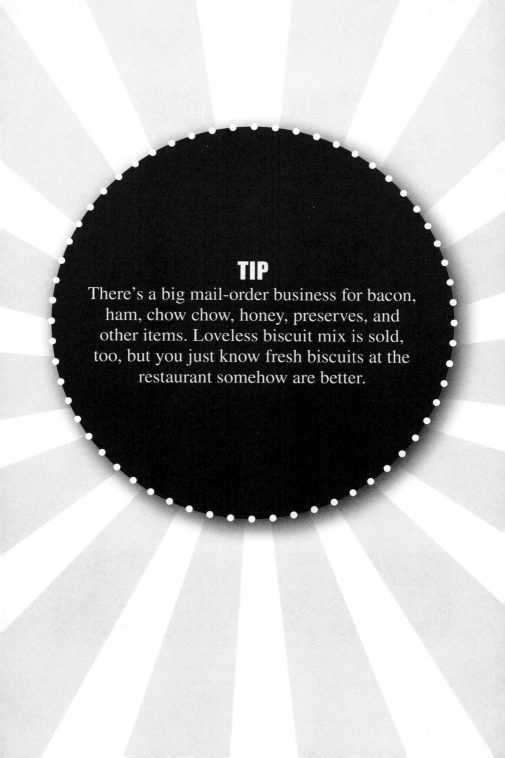

TIP

There's a big mail-order business for bacon, ham, chow chow, honey, preserves, and other items. Loveless biscuit mix is sold, too, but you just know fresh biscuits at the restaurant somehow are better.

SOAK UP SOME SUFFRAGETTE HISTORY
AT THE OAK BAR

Students of history know that Tennessee secured women's suffrage by pushing the Nineteenth Amendment to the U.S. Constitution over the top, but the students who earn an A are the ones who relax with a bourbon at the Oak Bar in the Hermitage Hotel to channel the debate. The elegant hotel, just steps from the state Capitol, was the headquarters for both the pro- and anti-suffrage camps, and it's a certainty that lively discussions occurred in the space later named the Oak Bar. Today, you can raise a toast to the Nineteenth Amendment and a second one to the Twenty-First Amendment, which ended Prohibition. In addition to all that bourbon, there's a nice menu in the Oak Bar, too.

231 Sixth Ave. N.
615-244-3121
capitolgrillenashville.com/oak-bar.asp

TIP
Women commonly peek into the men's room here. That's because this Art Deco-themed showplace with its leaded-glass tiles and terrazzo floors is in the Best Restrooms Hall of Fame. Honest, there really is a restroom hall of fame.

GRAB A BITE
AT TENNESSEE'S OLDEST RESTAURANT

Don't expect a wine list, white tablecloths, and a maître d' at Tennessee's oldest restaurant. They don't exist at Varallo's in the heart of downtown Nashville. Varallo's is a chili parlor, plain and simple, although there are biscuits at breakfast and a solid meat-and-three menu midday. Doors close mid-afternoon and don't open on Saturday or Sunday. Most famous is "chili three ways." That means meaty chili, snipped-up pieces of spaghetti, and bits of tamales. Nothing fancy here, folks. Good food and friendly hospitality have been served in copious quantities since 1907, making Varallo's a true culinary institution. The founder's great-grandson runs the show now, living up to the family motto: "It's always chili weather at Varallo's."

239 Fourth Ave. N.
615-256-1907
facebook.com/varallos

BATTLE OVER BARBECUE

The gift that keeps on giving is the discussion/debate/argument about who serves the best barbecue. Nobody wins, but that's okay. Here are four perennial favorites.

JACK'S BAR-B-QUE

Jack Cawthon, seldom seen without his riverboat gambler hat, was smoking pork and brisket on Lower Broadway before Lower Broadway was cool. He's still there, and in two other locations. His place on West Trinity Lane is a classic family barbecue destination.

Three locations
jacksbarbeque.com

PEG LEG PORKER

Pitmaster Carey Bringle, namesake of the Peg Leg Porker brand because of a losing battle with bone cancer, is one of the great personalities of the competitive barbecue world. He's even cooked at the James Beard House in New York. His one and only restaurant is at the edge of The Gulch.

903 Gleaves St.
615-829-6023
peglegporker.com

MARTIN'S BAR-B-QUE JOINT

Martin's started in rural/suburban Nolensville and then began opening other locations. There's even one downtown near the fancy Omni Hotel Nashville. Martin's brags on its whole-hog technique—and its coconut cake, pecan pie, and fudge pie.

Multiple locations
martinsbbqjoint.com

HOG HEAVEN

This Nashville institution in a building of no particular design would look perfect on some country road. There are a couple of picnic tables on a mostly screened-in patio, but it's mainly for carryout, which is fine, because picnic-worthy Centennial Park is its neighbor.

115 Twenty-Seventh Ave. N.
615-329-1234
hogheavenbbq.com

JOIN THE BURGER DEBATE

You can't win the "where's the best burger in town" debate, but you can hold your own with these nominees.

GABBY'S BURGERS & FRIES

Gabby's opened during the Great Recession and was an immediate hit. Burgers made with grass-fed beef and named for the owner's kids, an atmosphere that channels *Cheers* (but without the beer), sweet potato fries, and thick shakes are the winning combo here. It closes most days at 2:30 p.m.

493 Humphreys St.
615-773-3119
gabbysburgersandfries.com

BROWN'S DINER

Brown's really does resemble *Cheers* and has the oldest beer permit in Nashville to prove it—also legendary cheeseburgers, chili made daily, and Frito pie. The old portion, which defies gravity, is a streetcar and site of a well-worn fourteen-seat bar. Cold Bud and proximity to Music Row mean conversations are delicious, too.

2102 Blair Blvd.
615-269-5509
brownsdiner.com

DINO'S RESTAURANT

Even the owner doesn't understand how *Bon Appétit* picked Dino's for one of the three best burgers in America. Face it, Dino's is an East Nashville dive bar known best to the (very) late-night crowd. It doesn't even open until 4 p.m. except on weekends, when it serves a killer breakfast starting at noon.

411 Gallatin Ave.
615-226-3566
dinosnashville.com

TIP
Avoid fisticuffs by adding the Pharmacy Burger Parlor in East Nashville and Rotier's Restaurant near Vanderbilt to your gotta-try-'em list.

thepharmacynashville.com and rotiersrestaurant.com

INDULGE IN CHILLY NOSTALGIA
AT BOBBIE'S DAIRY DIP

Ignore the noisy traffic on busy Charlotte Avenue and take a nostalgic and potentially brain-freezing trip back in time at Bobbie's Dairy Dip. Bobbie's has been treating patrons to milkshakes, banana splits, burgers, and fries since 1951, and little has changed—although guacamole burgers and turkey hotdogs probably weren't on the original menu. Order at one window, pick up at another, and then perch on old picnic tables. There are more than twenty shake flavors, plus specialty shakes such as the Chubby Checker, the Barney Rubble, and the Elmer Fuddge. A good trivia game player will understand why the Joey Dee milkshake has Oreos and peppermint.

5301 Charlotte Ave.
615-463-8088
facebook.com/bobbiesdairydipcharlotteave

DINE WELL AND DO GOOD
AT THE CAFÉ AT THISTLE FARMS

There are two special outcomes from a visit to the Café at Thistle Farms—satisfaction from enjoying excellent food and knowledge that you've helped support a good cause. The café is one component of a nonprofit that heals, empowers, and employs women who have survived trafficking, prostitution, and addiction. Try the egg stack at breakfast (fried egg, pesto, avocado, and more on sourdough toast) or a grilled brie and basil sandwich at lunch. There's an afternoon tea service, too. Under the same roof is retail space for Thistle Farms' highly popular natural body products (soaps, lotions, fragrances, and such).

5122 Charlotte Ave.
615-953-6440
thecafeatthistlefarms.org

START A TACO TOUR
AT LA HACIENDA

La Hacienda began educating Nashville about authentic Mexican food almost four decades ago with a twenty-seat taco stand. That was a precursor to dozens of Mexican food establishments stretching for miles south along Nolensville Road. Check one out, go to the next one, drive a quarter-mile, and try another—but never forget La Hacienda, now a full-fledged, fast-paced restaurant with 130 seats, cold cerveza, sizzling fajita platters, breakfast all day, and lunch specials that leave change from a ten-dollar bill. President Obama even dropped by in 2014. Weekend specialties include *sopa de mariscos* (seafood stew with crab, octopus, shrimp, and scallops) and *birria de chivo* (goat meat served alone or in a stew). Next door is a sister business, a big-inventory Mexican food market with a full-service butcher shop and a bakery that cranks out a huge variety of breads and pastries. Its tortillas are sold in seven states.

2615 Nolensville Rd.
615-256-6142
lahanashville.com

TIP

Make Plaza Mariachi one of your taco tour stops. Multiple restaurants and businesses are inside a transformed Kroger supermarket. If you can't find something you like, you're just not cut out for international excitement. For details: plazamariachi.com

TRY THE PHO
AT KIEN GIANG

Long-time Nashvillians remember when the kitschy, but now retro, Omni Hut in Smyrna was the area's foray into international cuisine, with its Polynesian and slightly Asian menu. Nashville is far beyond that now, with cuisines from around the world. You need to dive in someplace, and a great (and inexpensive) start is a casual Vietnamese restaurant called Kien Giang just west of the Kroger on Charlotte Pike. Slurp some *pho*, try various *bánh mì* (Vietnamese sandwiches on pillow-soft bread), or go all out with a spicy *bò tái chanh* (rare sliced beef in lime juice sauce). Bring cash or a check — the owners are nearing three decades of success without taking credit cards. Kien Giang, by the way, is a province in Vietnam.

5825 Charlotte Pike
615-353-1250

WANDER AROUND FIVE POINTS
JUST FOR FUN

East Nashville's Five Points is a weird intersection of three streets, the kind that confuses drivers and confounds urban planners. It's the focal point of an area variously called hipster, funky, gentrified, and gritty. You can just call it fun. Enjoy anything chef Margot McCormack offers at Margot Café & Bar; play one of the three hundred board games at Game Point Café while sipping a fresh-roasted coffee from Bongo East; indulge your artistic side at the Art & Invention Gallery; find a special bottle at Woodland Wine Merchant; savor brunch at Marché Artisan Foods; buy some flashlight batteries at Cumberland Hardware because independent hardware stores need your support; get a bushwhacker at 3 Crow Bar, but remember that 151 rum packs a punch; or go wild at Gold Club Electric Tattoo. You get the idea.

Where Woodland St., Clearview Ave., and North Eleventh St. collide
visitmusiccity.com/visitors/neighborhoods/eastnashville

PACK YOUR PICNIC BASKET

AT THE NASHVILLE FARMERS' MARKET

This downtown treasure within sight of the Capitol offers more than fresh strawberries in spring, red tomatoes in summer, and sweet potatoes in autumn — and all the other farm-fresh goodies you can imagine through the growing season, when up to 150 farmers fill the Farm Sheds. There also are finished items such as honey, jams, jellies, and baked goods, plus some crafts and flea market merchandise. In the middle of it all is the Market House, with fourteen local restaurants (Asian, Mexican, Middle Eastern, Cajun, Jamaican, and more), an international market, and a few shops, including Batch, which emphasizes locally made items. Check out the Night Market, which supports a series of nonprofit groups and other community organizations the third Friday of every month.

900 Rosa L. Parks Blvd.
615-880-2001
nashvillefarmersmarket.org

HOP ON A BEER TOUR

While Tennessee's best-known alcoholic product is Jack Daniel's whiskey from eighty miles away in tiny Lynchburg (we're partial to the single-barrel product), Nashville is gaining a solid reputation for another beverage—craft beer. Nashville's beer scene, with almost two dozen sources of suds, is big enough to support a rolling brewery tour. Music City Brew Tours has ties to almost all local breweries. Each tour spotlights three breweries and includes ten to twelve sample tastings—plus a bus and a non-drinking driver between the stops. Light snacks are included on the bus, and tours can start with lunch or end with dinner (both on your own). Raise a toast to a nice education about hops, yeast, and good water!

615-485-1816
musiccitybrewtours.com

GET CAFFEINATED
ON A COFFEE TOUR

Even if you don't drink coffee, the aroma of roasting coffee beans is almost intoxicating, especially if a fresh pastry is tossed in for good measure. Nashville is fortunate to have a rich coffee culture and has plenty of independent caffeine suppliers that don't have "star" anywhere in their names.

Here are three mainstays to give you a wake-me-up
or a keep-me-going jolt.

BONGO JAVA

The original Bongo Java opened in East Nashville in 1993.
Others followed. International fame came in 1996 with the
discovery of the Nun Bun, a cinnamon roll that resembled
Mother Teresa. A sister establishment, Fido, straddles the line
between coffeehouse and casual restaurant.

Multiple locations
bongojava.com

BARISTA PARLOR

The first sleek and modern-looking Barista Parlor opened
in 2011 in East Nashville. Others followed in The Gulch
and Germantown, each one "seeking the betterment
of coffee for all mankind."

Multiple locations
baristaparlor.com

CREMA

Crema has its main location on Hermitage Avenue and an
outpost nearby at Pinewood Social, plus a great story of two
industrious owners with farming backgrounds who respect the
hard work of coffee growers in faraway places.

15 Hermitage Ave.
crema-coffee.com

GET THAT NASHVILLE BURN
WITH HOT CHICKEN

Nashville hot chicken is the stuff of legend, dating to the 1930s. Thornton Prince's lady friend wanted to get back at him for cattin' around, so she served him some fried chicken peppered up and spiced up enough to get his attention. Instead of gasping for air, Prince asked for more — and Nashville's trademark dish was born, as was a restaurant. To say today's Prince's Hot Chicken Shack is humble is an understatement. Expect to wait for your order of chicken, white bread, and dill pickle chips. Others have hopped on the hot chicken bandwagon with various degrees of heat, but at Prince's, go with the mild version — at least the first time.

123 Ewing Dr.
615-226-9442

5814 Nolensville Rd.
615-810-9388

princeshotchicken.com

TIP

The free-admission Music City Hot
Chicken Festival on July 4 at East Park
will put your taste buds to a serious test.
Hattie B's, Pepperfire, and others are gaining
fans. Proceeds benefit the Friends of
Shelby Park & Bottoms. For details:
hot-chicken.com/festival

ATTEND A TOMATO PARTY

You say to-MAY-to, I say to-MAH-to. You say tomato is a fruit, I say it's a vegetable. That's all irrelevant for one glorious weekend every August when the noble tomato exists only as the object of everyone's affection at the Tomato Art Festival in East Nashville. This community celebration grew like a sprawling 'mater vine from the Art & Invention Gallery's promotion of a 2004 art show about the wonderful fruit/vegetable. Attendance now exceeds fifty thousand tomato fanatics, who come for the Tomato 5K Run, a Bloody Mary contest (of course), the Tomato King and Queen Contest, the Tomato Parade, and other frivolities. It's a very costume-friendly event, so you'll blend right in if you come dressed as a tomato-and-mayonnaise-on-white-bread sandwich.

Throughout the Five Points Neighborhood
1160 Woodland St.
615-266-2070
tomatoartfest.com

SOBER UP (OR FILL UP)
AT THE HERMITAGE CAFE

The Hermitage Cafe has perhaps the most unusual restaurant schedule in town. It opens at 10 p.m. every night and closes at 1:30 p.m. the next afternoon. In those hours, it serves a cross-section of the night-owl crowd (some in, shall we say, colorful professions), revelers who really, really need some food in their stomachs after too much honky tonk time, and some folks who simply want a great breakfast that includes the cafe's famous biscuits and gravy or a meat-and-three meal. Check out the "Carnivore Omelet"—it's four eggs, cheese, bacon, ham, and sausage, plus home fries and biscuits. That should hold you until 10 p.m. rolls around again. Every cab, Lyft, and Uber driver knows the way to the Hermitage Cafe. Bring cash; no credit cards here.

71 Hermitage Ave.
615-254-8871
hermitagecafetn.com

MUSIC AND ENTERTAINMENT

GO GRAND
AT THE GRAND OLE OPRY

In some ways, the Grand Ole Opry is as flashy a concert experience as you'll ever have, but it still proudly shows its roots as exactly what it is, a live radio show. Yes, what you see, including the novelty of square dancers performing for listeners who can't see them, is booming out over the 50,000-watt signal of WSM-AM, just as it did when it launched in 1925 (although then with a signal not as big). It's live, it's unrehearsed, those really are commercials (Goo Goo Clusters, Martha White Flour, Goody's Headache Powder, and Cracker Barrel among them through the years), and Opry members talk lovingly about being part of the Opry "family." See the show at the Grand Ole Opry House (4,400 seats) in the suburbs or at the Ryman Auditorium (space for 2,300 rear ends on hardwood church pews) downtown.

2804 Opryland Dr.
615-871-OPRY (6779)
opry.com

JUMP ON IN
WITH THE TIME JUMPERS

When you have to prove to someone that Nashville is eaten up with stellar studio musicians, take your skeptical friend to 3rd & Lindsley on Monday night. That's when The Time Jumpers assemble. You don't necessarily know *who* you are going to see, but you absolutely know *what* you're going to get—extraordinary musicianship, great singing, wonderful camaraderie, and cold beer. Mondays, often slow for these ten super musicians, were when they started gathering to jam at the Station Inn bluegrass club in 1998. Pretty soon, they had fans. And Grammy nominations. Their venue now is the much larger 3rd & Lindsley, a club whose lineup you should monitor regardless. Among The Time Jumpers are "Ranger Doug" Green from Riders in the Sky, steel guitar virtuoso Paul Franklin, fiddlers Larry Franklin and Joe Spivey, and a budding vocalist and guitar picker named Vince Gill.

818 Third Ave. S.
615-259-9891
3rdandlindsley.com
thetimejumpers.com

CLAP LOUDLY
AT *MUSIC CITY ROOTS*

When you applaud, whistle, and cheer at a performance of *Music City Roots*, your enthusiasm appears nationwide. That's because this two-hour celebration of Americana music, which originated in 2009, airs on more than 60 percent of the nation's public television stations. It is webcast live and is in radio syndication, too. The weekly shows energize a six-hundred-seat venue in the heart of Nashville and spotlight the city's amazing musical variety. Jim Lauderdale, who personifies Americana music to many, is the musical host for performers such as Emmylou Harris, Rodney Crowell, Billy Joe Shaver, Margo Price, Sturgill Simpson, and the Earls of Leicester. Like Americana music itself, lineups are a mixing bowl of folk, bluegrass, rhythm and blues, jazz, and other styles. Every show concludes with an all-hands-on-deck jam. Don't even think about leaving early.

Sixth Ave. S. and Peabody St.
615-669-1627
musiccityroots.com

TIP
AMERICANAFEST is a weeklong
celebration for the music industry and fans
alike. About five hundred performances in
sixty venues fill six nights in September.
It all culminates in an awards show at the
Ryman Auditorium. For details:
americanamusic.org/about-americanafest

SHHHH!

AT THE BLUEBIRD CAFE

No "listening room" anywhere is more famous than The Bluebird Cafe, and that was true before TV's *Nashville* so widely exposed the concept of a club where patrons actually pay attention to performers. The "Shhhh! policy" is real — and enforced. Nashville is a songwriters' town, and a Bluebird Cafe visit lets you hear up-and-coming writers as well as established hit makers. The norm has three or four songwriters in the center of the tiny club (ninety seats) taking turns with their songs and accompanying each other instrumentally and with harmony vocals. This Green Hills strip mall treasure is in the care of the Nashville Songwriters Association International. Don't expect to show up and get a seat, although limited walkup seating is available for early shows. Arrive at least an hour before late shows for a chance at unclaimed seats. Follow the strict reservation protocol for a true Nashville treat.

4104 Hillsboro Pike
615-383-1461
bluebirdcafe.com

TIP

Although online reservations are
snapped up almost immediately,
the 9:30 p.m. Monday show is first-come,
first-seated, and there are ten to twelve
church pew seats for walkups at early
shows. Gamble if you want.

GET INTIMATE
WITH A SONGWRITER

The Bluebird Cafe doesn't exactly suck all the oxygen out of the room, but it's far from the only place in town to have an intimate, but purely platonic, relationship with a songwriter. Nashville is absolutely the epicenter of America's songwriting, and that is proven every night of the week in venues all over town. You'll find everything from an open mic night to special performances by songwriters with multiple Grammy Awards. The Tin Pan South Songwriters Festival every spring is a five-day blowout (ten venues, two shows a night, four hundred songwriters) for a full-immersion experience. To get sprinkled instead of dunked, visit venues such as Douglas Corner Cafe, The Listening Room Cafe, the Commodore Grille, and Belcourt Taps.

TIP
Wouldn't it be nice if there were a central place to search for a songwriter event? Well, there is. It's a nonprofit website called NowPlayingNashville.com, an initiative of the Community Foundation of Middle Tennessee. Use it for songwriter events and just about every other conceivable form of entertainment. For details: nowplayingnashville.com

BE A HONKY TONK MAN
(OR GAL)

Give in to the urge to channel Johnny Horton or Dwight Yoakam (Horton wrote the classic "I'm a Honky Tonk Man," and he and Yoakam had hits with it decades apart) and explore the seemingly unending collection of beer-serving-live-music-playing-no-longer-smoky honky tonks on Lower Broadway. Some have great stories (Tootsie's Orchid Lounge was a hangout for Opry members when the Opry was across the alley at the Ryman Auditorium), and others sport A-list country music artists' names. Among anchor establishments in addition to Tootsie's (which has an outpost at Nashville's airport) are Legends Corner, The Second Fiddle, Layla's, The Stage, and Robert's Western World. It's impossible to beat a good band and a Recession Special at Robert's. That's a fried bologna sandwich, chips, and a cold Pabst Blue Ribbon Beer for five dollars, tax included. Remember to tip your server and the band.

Broadway between Second and Fifth Aves.
visitmusiccity.com/visitors/honkytonkhighway

ENJOY 'THAT HIGH LONESOME SOUND'
AT THE STATION INN

Ask any bluegrass band in the world where it wants to play in Nashville, and the answer will be the Station Inn, a two-hundred-seat club that thrives on bluegrass and roots music in a nondescript one-story building in The Gulch. Bill Monroe, the Father of Bluegrass Music himself, would sometimes come over after appearing at the Grand Ole Opry, watch from the back of the house, and then stroll through the audience and ask whether he could play in. That's like God's asking whether He can come to Wednesday night meeting with you. When the Station Inn moved to The Gulch in 1978, the neighborhood was, shall we say, rough, but bluegrass pickers and fans didn't care. Fancy hotels, restaurants, and condos now tower over the Station Inn, but bluegrass pickers and fans don't mind, although parking has gotten tougher.

402 Twelfth Ave. S.
615-255-3307
stationinn.com

TIP

Wicked parody, risqué lyrics, and some exquisite comedic timing are hallmarks of the three-person *Doyle & Debbie Show*, a frequent Tuesday feature at the Station Inn. Beware if you're easily offended. For details: doyleanddebbie.com

STEEP YOURSELF
IN COUNTRY MUSIC

The Country Music Hall of Fame and Museum has a big story to tell—and you'll enjoy it even if you don't know much about country music or even if you say you don't like it. This massive facility has two million artifacts (not all visible at one time, of course) that tell the story of Nashville's special calling card through vintage video, recorded sound, famous instruments, manuscripts, and even Elvis Presley's "Solid Gold Cadillac." Limited-engagement exhibitions complement the core exhibit, *Sing Me Back Home*. No wonder it's called "the Smithsonian of country music." Plan on at least two or three hours, but realize your ticket is good all day. That means you can dive into a nearby honky tonk for a cold beer and a tear-jerking song and return for more museum exploration.

222 Fifth Ave. S.
615-416-2001
countrymusichalloffame.org

TIP
If you have a Nashville library card, ask about the Community Counts Passport that provides two free museum admissions. Each branch has a limited number to check out—just like a book.

SEE WHERE HITS WERE MADE
AT HISTORIC RCA STUDIO B

The only way to see Music Row's Historic RCA Studio B, one of the most storied recording studios in the world, is with an add-on ticket to the Country Music Hall of Fame and Museum, but it's worth it. Studio B nurtured "the Nashville Sound" and was where thirty-five thousand songs, one thousand Top 10 American hits, and forty million-selling songs were recorded. Artists whose spirits and good vibes fill the studio include Eddy Arnold, Waylon Jennings, Dolly Parton, Jim Reeves, Willie Nelson, the Everly Brothers, Roy Orbison, and that fellow from Memphis named Elvis Presley. He recorded more than two hundred songs here. Close your eyes, and you may hear him singing "How Great Thou Art" or "It's Now or Never."

Access from the Country Music Hall of Fame and Museum
222 Fifth Ave. S.
615-416-2001
countrymusichalloffame.org

GET THE BEAT
AT THE MUSICIANS HALL OF FAME

The unsung heroes of the music world (pun intended) are the talented studio musicians who create the environments where singers can add their touches to a song. The Musicians Hall of Fame and Museum addresses that anonymity. The museum is downtown and slightly off the beaten path in the aging, but quite serviceable, Municipal Auditorium. Nashville's famous studio musicians are honored, of course, but this is not a Nashville-only museum. It tells a national story and also puts the spotlight on other powerhouse music cities such as Memphis, Los Angeles, Muscle Shoals, and Detroit. Guitarist Duane Eddy, one of the few musicians in this group with a public persona, narrates an excellent film in which he explains how super-talented musicians can turn "three minutes in a closed room into a lifetime of memories." You'll recognize what he means as you hum or sing your way through every exhibit.

401 Gay St.
615-244-3263
musicianshalloffame.com

SWING LOW
WITH THE FISK JUBILEE SINGERS

One of Music City's greatest musical stories is the Fisk Jubilee Singers, the a cappella ensemble that saved a struggling college created just after the Civil War to educate freed slaves. The group formed in 1871 to tour and raise funds for Fisk University, introducing slave songs to the world and preserving an American musical tradition. Initial results were rocky, but a fire had been lit. The Fisk Jubilee singers went to the White House and on to Europe, performing for Queen Victoria in London in 1873. America honored them in 2008 with the National Medal of Arts. Today's Fisk Jubilee Singers carry on a great tradition, so watch for a public performance. Grab a ticket if you see a booking, especially if it's at the acoustically marvelous Ryman Auditorium.

fiskjubileesingers.org

LEARN ABOUT SONGWRITERS
AT THIS HALL OF FAME

The Nashville Songwriters Hall of Fame isn't a grand edifice attracting throngs of fans daily. It's actually pretty small and not even a freestanding building, but it still can command considerable time filled with comments such as, "Wow! I didn't know Gene Autry wrote 'Here Comes Santa Claus'" and "Why is Chuck Berry honored here?" This hall of fame is a fancy gallery of artifacts and electronics on the second floor of the Music City Center, the city's gigantic convention center. Treasures to behold include a handwritten letter Hank Williams wrote to his publisher doubting the quality of "I Saw the Light" and a first draft of Paul Craft's "Dropkick Me, Jesus (Through the Goalposts of Life)." Chuck Berry is in the mix because songs he wrote were hits for country legends Marty Robbins, Conway Twitty, and George Jones. Admission is free.

201 Fifth Ave. S.
615-292-5804
nashvillesongwritersfoundation.com

TIP

Stroll around Music City Walk of Fame Park, just down Demonbreun St. from the Music City Center. In-ground plaques honor artists and industry professionals with special connections to Nashville. If you're lucky, be a spectator when a new member's plaque is installed.

GET CULTURED
AT THE TENNESSEE PERFORMING ARTS CENTER

A Broadway show in Nashville definitely means something other than a country band blaring in a Lower Broadway honky tonk. What it really means is seeing an honest-to-goodness Broadway touring production at the Tennessee Performing Arts Center (TPAC), a three-theater facility that adds immeasurable class to an otherwise mundane state office building at the corner of Deaderick Street and Sixth Avenue North. Broadway shows and all manner of other performances such as concerts, comedy acts, and lectures keep the theaters buzzing. The performance spaces are named for Tennessee's U.S. presidents (Andrew Jackson, James K. Polk, and Andrew Johnson) and range from 256 to 2,472 seats. TPAC also is home to three resident artistic companies—Nashville Opera, Nashville Ballet, and Nashville Repertory Theatre. There's always a reason to go to TPAC.

505 Deaderick St.
615-782-4040
tpac.org

CHEER WITH CHILDLIKE WONDER
AT THE NASHVILLE CHILDREN'S THEATRE

When Nashville's Junior League staged *Aladdin and His Wonderful Lamp* in 1931, it is doubtful anyone envisioned it as the start of what has become America's oldest professional theater for young audiences. Nashville Children's Theatre productions were staged in various locations for many years, including the Belcourt Theatre (page 58), before settling into a multifaceted home just seven blocks and a world away from Lower Broadway's honky tonks. Its productions are aimed at various age levels, and it even has an incubator program called the Hatchery to develop new plays for young audiences. Treat your own kids, a grandchild, a favorite niece, or a neighbor family with youngsters to an NCT show — and don't forget your own ticket.

25 Middleton St.
615-252-4675 (box office)
nashvillechildrenstheatre.org

HOWL
AT A FULL MOON PICKIN' PARTY

Bill Monroe — creator of bluegrass music, member of the Grand Ole Opry, member of the Country Music Hall of Fame — must smile down from heaven when a Full Moon Pickin' Party cranks up in Warner Park. The Friday closest to the full moon from May through October brings out bluegrass pickers and bluegrass fans for a night of hot licks, musical camaraderie, and appreciation of Mr. Monroe's "high lonesome sound." In addition to three headline acts on the main stage, there are impromptu jams with people who have brought their own guitars, banjos, dulcimers, bass fiddles, and other acoustical instruments. The parties are at the Warner Park Equestrian Center and are fundraisers for Percy Warner Park and Edwin Warner Park. Bring a picnic if you want; tickets include water, soft drinks, and (this is true) up to four beers.

2500 Old Hickory Blvd.
615-370-8053
warnerparks.org/programs-events

TIP

This music concept is so good that it spread to the opposite side of town. Check out the Cornelia Fort Pickin' Party four times in summer and early autumn at the Cornelia Fort Airpark, antique airplane included. Proceeds benefit Shelby Park and Bottoms. For details: friendsofshelby.org/pickin_parties

GET TOASTY
AT LIVE ON THE GREEN

Summertime heat aside, six cool evenings of free entertainment await you at Live on the Green every August and September. Lightning 100, one of the nation's top independent radio stations, presents concerts on three Thursdays in August and then a three-day blowout on the Thursday, Friday, and Saturday of Labor Day weekend. The setting is Public Square Park, an open expanse that has the Metro Courthouse as a backdrop. Lightning 100 is a rock and Americana station, and Live on the Green artists have included Ben Harper, Sheryl Crow, Alabama Shakes, and Cage The Elephant. Concerts attract around fifteen thousand fans. Bring a blanket or a folding chair and enjoy this family-friendly outdoor party.

Third Ave. N. and Union St.
615-242-5600
liveonthegreen.com

TIP
Cheap parking (five dollars) is available in a garage under the park, and if you have cash to burn, there are VIP tickets that provide up-front views, beer, wine, catering, and air-conditioned flushable restroom facilities.

JOIN THE SING-ALONG
AT CMA FEST

If you've ever wanted to sing your favorite country songs along with fifty thousand sweaty people on a hot summer night, Nashville has the event for you—CMA Fest, "the ultimate country music fan experience." It's been a Music City fixture early every June since 1972 when the Opry Trust Fund originated it for an audience of five thousand people at the Municipal Auditorium. How quaint and modest that sounds now. Today's four-day, multivenue festival pulls in about ninety thousand fans for nightly huge-production shows at Nissan Stadium, daytime concerts along the downtown riverfront, and the glory of air-conditioned events inside the Music City Center. Much of the activity is ticketed, but there are ways to be royally entertained for free. A network TV special comes out of every CMA Fest, but watching the special doesn't earn you bragging rights as a CMA Fest veteran.

Nissan Stadium, Music City Center, other venues
cmaworld.com/cma-music-festival

GET AN EARFUL
AT MUSICIANS CORNER

London's Hyde Park has Speakers' Corner, so Nashville's Centennial Park, of course, has Musicians Corner, adding to the city's amazing array of live music opportunities. Performers (new, established, and legendary) play on two outdoor stages in Nashville's most famous park. Events happen Friday and Saturday evenings in May and June and again in the fall. Just bring a lawn chair or a blanket and perhaps a picnic basket. The Conservancy for the Parthenon and Centennial Park, the park's "friends" organization, is the producer, and it books top-caliber performers. Among them: Vince Gill, Emmylou Harris, Chris Stapleton, the Blind Boys of Alabama, the Fairfield Four, Preservation Hall Jazz Band, Jars of Clay, St. Paul & The Broken Bones, and the Secret Sisters — 1,200 in the first eight years alone. Shows are free, and even though this is a city park, craft beer and cocktails are available. What's not to like?

Centennial Park
615-862-6810
musicianscornernashville.com

YUK IT UP
AT A COMEDY CLUB

Standup comic Killer Beaz performs nationwide, but he especially enjoys making people laugh at Zanies Comedy Night Club on Eighth Avenue South because he can go to his own house after his show. "Save up!" is one of this Nashville resident's catch phrases, but you usually don't need all that much coin to get some laughs in Music City. For a medium-sized city marinated in music, Nashville's comedy scene is solid. Beyond nightly zaniness at Zanies, check out the Third Coast Comedy Club in Marathon Village for improv and sketch comedy, Bobby's Idle Hour Tavern for Monday night frivolities, and the East Room on Gallatin Pike for open mic Tuesdays. Every spring, big-name performers flood in for the Nashville Comedy Festival in locations including the Bridgestone Arena, TPAC, the War Memorial Auditorium, and the Ryman Auditorium.

TIP
To track down comedy opportunities, which are scattered all over town, lean on NowPlayingNashville.com, the region's comprehensive entertainment information source.

RUN A MUSEUM MARATHON
TO SEE JOHNNY CASH, PATSY CLINE, AND GEORGE JONES

This is a marathon of time, not distance, because these three museums are within blocks of each other. Count on spending hours to absorb the life stories of these entertainment giants. Yes, these are tourist attractions, but they are museums first.

GEORGE JONES MUSEUM

Jones led one of the most action-packed lives imaginable. Huge hits, *Louisiana Hayride* co-billing with Elvis Presley, Grand Ole Opry membership, rocky marriages, substance abuse, redemption, and more hits — including the greatest country song ever, "He Stopped Loving Her Today." True fans understand the John Deere lawnmower on display. (Hint: If your wife has taken the car keys, you still can drive the lawnmower to the liquor store.) The museum and related attractions occupy a historic warehouse. The rooftop bar has cold beer, live music, and Cumberland River views. Jones would approve.

128 Second Ave. N., 615-818-0128
georgejones.com/museum/

JOHNNY CASH MUSEUM

This gem is in another converted industrial building and tells a story just as big. Its huge collection belongs to a fan named Bill Miller, who at age nine met Cash. From the stage, Cash handed him the harmonica he had just played, and Miller collected Cash memorabilia for the next forty-six years. The museum honors Cash's music along with his movie and TV work. (Did you know he got equal billing with Kirk Douglas in *A Gunfight*?) Also recognized for its importance to country music is ABC's *The Johnny Cash Show*, which was produced in the nearby Ryman Auditorium.

119 Third Ave. S., 615-256-1777
johnnycashmuseum.com

PATSY CLINE MUSEUM

One street-level entrance serves both the Johnny Cash Museum and the Patsy Cline Museum. Don't miss either one. Cline broke ground for women in country music. She rose from humble beginnings, made a splash on national TV (*Arthur Godfrey's Talent Scouts*), is said to be the only person bold enough to ask to become a Grand Ole Opry member, scored hit after hit (including several that crossed over to pop), and was the first female country singer to headline in Las Vegas. Her life ended in a tragic airplane crash, but the museum doesn't dwell on that. Instead, it leaves you admiring the artistry that delivered a "greatest hits" album that was on Billboard's charts for 722 weeks.

119 Third Ave. S., 615-454-4722
patsymuseum.com

HAVE A CINEMATIC EXPERIENCE
AT THE BELCOURT

You don't go to the Belcourt Theatre to see the latest Marvel Comics movie sequel. You go to the Belcourt to soak in a classic film (*Casablanca*, perhaps), to see this year's Oscar-nominated documentaries, or to see that independent film that just won't appear elsewhere in Nashville. The Belcourt, Nashville's nonprofit film center, is a two-screen gem (plus a thirty-five-seat screening room for special uses) in Hillsboro Village that oozes history and nostalgia. It opened in 1925 with eight hundred seats for silent movies, was home to the Grand Ole Opry from 1934 to 1936, and survived the movie industry's myriad changes over the decades. It presents three hundred films a year (2,300 screenings), and the array makes your head spin—just like the reels of the giant projector overhead. Everything got totally spiffed up in 2016 with a $5 million renovation.

2102 Belcourt Ave.
615-846-3150
belcourt.org

JUST PICK SOMETHING TO DO
AT FONTANEL

When superstar Barbara Mandrell sold Fontanel, her super home in the woods about fifteen minutes northwest of downtown, she probably never dreamed it would become the core element of an attraction where you can — get ready — tour the thirty-three-thousand-square-foot log home, attend a concert in a 4,500-seat amphitheater among the trees, stay at a six-suite B&B that began as a Southern Living Idea House, zip through the treetops on a canopy tour, sample rums and Tennessee whiskey distilled on site, visit a wine tasting room, dine on Italian cuisine, or enjoy a free family-friendly Back Porch Concert on summer Thursdays. That's most, but not all, of what goes on at Fontanel.

4125 White's Creek Pike
615-724-1600
fontanel.com

KEEP THE VIBE ALIVE
IN PRINTERS ALLEY

Downtown's Printers Alley is one of America's storied entertainment districts. It really is an alley, and it really has roots in printing and publishing dating into the 1800s. Its entertainment fame evolved in the 1940s, when Nashville's entertainers and musicians wanted places to play, and Nashville residents and visitors wanted places to eat and drink, even though liquor by the drink wasn't legal until 1968. Club owners had workarounds for the booze, and entertainment always was in demand. Who performed? Try Etta James, Chet Atkins, Jerry Lee Lewis, Boots Randolph, Waylon Jennings, Andy Griffith, stripper Heaven Lee, and many more. Printers Alley waxed and waned over the decades, but establishments such as Skull's Rainbow Room, Bourbon Street Blues and Boogie Bar, Fleet Street Pub, and Ms. Kelli's Karaoke keep the vibe alive. There's even a 169-room hotel, the Dream Nashville.

Printers Alley
(between Third and Fourth Aves. N. and Union and Commerce Sts.)
nashvilledowntown.com/go/printers-alley

STAY COOL
INSIDE THE GAYLORD OPRYLAND RESORT

It seems that absolutely everyone has attended a convention at the Gaylord Opryland Resort, but if you've not stayed in this sprawling hotel either for business or leisure, it's a must-see. You could label it the "Hotel That Grew Like Topsy." It was big when it opened in 1977 with six hundred rooms, but three expansions boosted the room count to 2,888 and created nine acres of climate-controlled gardens, meaning that even if the weather outside is frightful, it's perpetually spring inside. The largest of three massive gardens covers almost five acres, and it includes an indoor river that was christened with samples of rivers from around the world. The hotel's well-traveled friends used miniature Jack Daniel's bottles to mail the water to Nashville. And you can't imagine how this showplace looks at Christmas.

2800 Opryland Dr.
615-889-1000
gaylordhotels.com

TIP
The hotel's heritage includes WSM-AM, the Grand Ole Opry station. That explains the showcase studio just off the Magnolia Lobby. Peer inside to see broadcasters such as Country Radio Hall of Fame members Bill Cody and Eddie Stubbs at work.

SPORTS AND RECREATION

HIT A NASHVILLE SOUNDS HOMERUN

The only "minor league" aspect of a Nashville Sounds baseball game is the fact that the team is in the AAA Pacific Coast League. Everything else is strictly big league. It's so good that Nashville topped a 159-city ranking of minor league game-day experiences and ambience. The Sounds' game features the ten-thousand-seat First Tennessee Park, a guitar-shaped scoreboard with a 4,200-square-foot LED screen, a 360-degree game-viewing experience, Nashville hot chicken at the concession stands, and promotions galore. The downtown stadium offers a great view of the city skyline, and numerous bars and restaurants are nearby for pre- and post-game entertainment. A bonus: attend the City of Hope Celebrity Softball Game during June's CMA Fest that pits country music stars against each other, some of whom are very, very serious about winning.

19 Junior Gilliam Way
615-690-4487
nashvillesounds.com

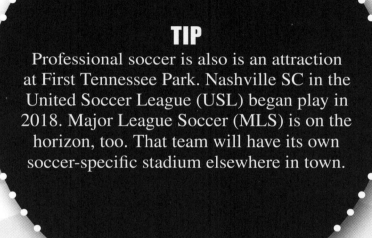

TIP

Professional soccer is also is an attraction at First Tennessee Park. Nashville SC in the United Soccer League (USL) began play in 2018. Major League Soccer (MLS) is on the horizon, too. That team will have its own soccer-specific stadium elsewhere in town.

BARE YOUR FANG FINGERS
AT THE NASHVILLE PREDATORS

Skeptics wondered whether the NHL could succeed in the football-crazy South, but the Nashville Predators skated into Nashville in 1998, proved them wrong, and taught broadcasters how to pronounce the names of Finnish, Russian, and Czech players. A Predators game is a Music City spectacle. A live band performs between periods, every national anthem singer is stellar (sometimes it really is an A-list country star), the team mascot rappels from the rafters, and the crowd noise rattles the roof. (It's okay to bring earplugs.) Let your hair down and join the chants from the rowdies in Section 303. You'll soon beg for the visiting team to draw a penalty so you can raise two fingers on each hand and holler "Fang Fingers!" as the offender enters the penalty box.

501 Broadway
615-770-7825
nhl.com/predators

TIP

Look for a display case on the 100 Level that contains a nine-inch fang from a *Smilodon*, a prehistoric saber-toothed cat. It was found in the 1971 excavation of a nearby building and became the inspiration for the hockey team's name.

CHEER FOR THE TITANS

The Tennessee Titans bring National Football League pageantry and bruise-producing action to Nashville at least eight times a year, ten if you add two exhibition games, and maybe more if the muscular athletes make the playoffs. The action is inside the 69,143-seat Nissan Stadium that sits conspicuously on the east bank of the Cumberland River just across from the honky tonks and restaurants of Lower Broadway. Scoring a ticket usually isn't all that difficult, and before each season begins, there's a way to see the sweaty behemoths for free. That's because some summer practices are open to spectators at Saint Thomas Sports Park in MetroCenter. You might snag an autograph there, too.

One Titans Way
615-565-4200 (ticket office)
titansonline.com

RUN, JOG, OR TROT
FOR 13.1 OR 26.2 MILES

The start of the St. Jude Rock 'n' Roll Nashville Marathon and Half-Marathon is a spectacle worthy of a classic Cecil B. DeMille movie or a modern action thriller. Approximately thirty-five thousand otherwise sane people pack onto Broadway on an April morning and proceed to lope through downtown, out Music Row, across the Cumberland River, and to points beyond before crossing the finish line at Nissan Stadium. This is Music City, so of course there are live bands all along the route, plus cheering fans and curious onlookers. It's a sight to behold, either as participant or spectator. If you just watch, wave an encouraging sign. Our favorite: "I Don't Know You, But I'll Cheer for You Anyway." One reward for runners is a concert at Bridgestone Arena by a major act.

runrockroll.com/nashville

WATCH BRUINS AND BISONS
BATTLE IT OUT

After a chilly Nashville winter, there's little better than soaking in some natural vitamin D at a college baseball game. The atmosphere is casual, the competition is pure, and the price is modest. Opportunities abound, and one of the best rivalries is between Belmont University and Lipscomb University, institutions separated by only about two miles and a few points of theology. (Belmont has Southern Baptist roots, and Lipscomb is a Church of Christ school.) Belmont's Bruins play at E.S. Rose Park, a Metro Nashville Parks facility enhanced with $8 million from the university, and Lipscomb's Bisons play at Ken Dugan Field, named for a coach who notched more than one thousand wins over thirty-six seasons. Belmont and Lipscomb duke it out in basketball season, too, in what's called the Battle of the Boulevard.

<table>
<tr><td>Belmont Baseball</td><td>Lipscomb Baseball</td></tr>
<tr><td>1000 Edgehill Ave.</td><td>4103 Granny White Pike</td></tr>
<tr><td>615-460-6420</td><td>615-966-1000</td></tr>
<tr><td>belmont.prestosports.com</td><td>lipscombsports.com</td></tr>
</table>

TIP

For some Southeastern Conference action, head to Hawkins Field at Vanderbilt University. The Commodores are regulars in NCAA tournament action and were national champions in 2014. For details: vucommodores.com

GO WILD
AT THE NASHVILLE ZOO AT GRASSMERE

Some of the critters at the Nashville Zoo at Grassmere are just too cute for words—and that's just considering the toddlers and their grandparents who stroll along the winding paths of this one-hundred-acre attraction. More cuteness lies in red pandas, meerkats, Mexican spider monkeys, and ring-tailed lemurs, just four of the zoo's 365 species. Of course, there are some residents with countenances only their mothers could love (just try to get a smiling photo of a southern white rhino, a Goliath bird-eating tarantula, or a short-tailed, leaf-nosed bat). The open-air habitats and shaded walkways make the zoo particularly enjoyable for visitors, and the zoo's breeding and conservation programs make it special for animals from many faraway places. Among the newest are Andean bears from Peru.

3777 Nolensville Pike
615-833-1534
nashvillezoo.org

TIP
If anatomy, dinosaurs, moonwalks, tornadoes, astronomy, and other science topics grab you more than those cute animals at the zoo—or if the weather drives you indoors—head for the Adventure Science Center. For details: adventuresci.org

TAKE A LAZY FLOAT
ON THE HARPETH RIVER

You could put a canoe into the Harpeth River and float all the way to New Orleans (that's if you turn left at the Cumberland, left at the Ohio, and left at the Mississippi), but you don't want to do that. What you do want to do is rent a canoe from Tip-a-Canoe or another outfitter for a point-to-point float on this easy Class I river. Its surroundings are rural rather than wild, a pleasant contrast from nearby developed Nashville. The Harpeth is quite popular with canoeists and kayakers, so you're unlikely ever to be truly alone. One popular float includes the Narrows of the Harpeth, a five-mile stretch where the river makes a huge bend and comes back within a quarter-mile of itself. Harpeth River State Park has nine access points along forty miles of the river. Use sunscreen!

Harpeth River State Park
615-952-2099
tnstateparks.com/about/harpeth-river

Tip-a-Canoe
800-550-5810
tip-a-canoe.com

ROLL AROUND TOWN
ON A BICYCLE

Remember when you were a kid and could hop on your bike and pedal off to a friend's house to play? Modern-day bike sharing can bring that memory to life if you pick up a bike from one of approximately three dozen B-cycle racks scattered through many parts of town. You don't have to return to the rack where you started, meaning you could pedal out of Germantown, ditch your bike at Five Points in East Nashville for lunch, find another rack, get a second bike, and pedal out to Centennial Park. Your options are almost innumerable. B-cycles have baskets, front and rear lights, and, yes, a bell. Just like when you were a kid.

nashville.bicycle.com

TIP
Bicyclists love Nashville's greenway system, and Bike the Greenway at Wave Country in Donelson has rental bikes for exploring Shelby Bottoms in one direction or riding to Percy Priest Dam in the other. For details: bikethegreenway.net

GET DRESSY
AT THE IROQUOIS STEEPLECHASE

The one-day Iroquois Steeplechase every May attracts two types, the horse set and the party set. Some people might actually be in both camps. For some, this springtime tradition since 1941 is about top-caliber racing horses. For others, this is an excuse to dress up in spring finery, flirt, drink outdoors, and see and be seen. It's part race, part fashion show, and part society soiree, a day for big flower-topped hats, sundresses, seersucker suits, bowties, and suspenders. Veteran attendees also know it's a day for sunscreen, patience getting back to your car, and raingear. The three-mile track is in Percy Warner Park, and attendance can approach twenty-five thousand. General admission is only twenty dollars, but you can pay many multiples of that to get fancy food and other benefits.

2500 Old Hickory Blvd.
615-591-2991
iroquoissteeplechase.org

WALK IN THE WOODS,
BUT STAY IN THE CITY

A lake built to provide water to steam-driven locomotives a century ago was the genesis for Tennessee's first state natural area. What's especially notable about Radnor Lake State Park is that its 1,332 acres are a wilderness oasis not eight miles from the state Capitol. Forward-thinking nature lovers bought the lake just before a two-hundred-home subdivision was to pop up around the lake and on surrounding ridges. Quiet reigns today, unless you count the screech of an osprey, the splash of a beaver, or the rustling of leaves caused by a passing deer. There are six miles of trails, an aviary education center for non-releasable birds (including a bald eagle), a fifty-seat amphitheater for ranger-led programs, and benches for silent solitude. Hiking, bird watching, and nature photography are the big attractions.

1160 Otter Creek Rd.
615-373-3467
tnstateparks.com/parks/about/radnor-lake

TIP
Find more nature diagonally across Nashville in Beaman Park, a city-owned 1,693-acre preserve of ridges, valleys, forest, and creeks. Assets include a nature center, five miles of trails, and frequent programs, including night hikes by the full moon. For details: nashville.gov/parks-and-recreation/nature-centers-and-natural-areas

LEARN TENNESSEE'S STORIES
AT BICENTENNIAL CAPITOL MALL

Few people expect to find a state park in the middle of the city, but Tennessee created one to mark its bicentennial in 1996. It is the Bicentennial Capitol Mall State Park, all nineteen acres of it, and it takes full advantage of the only unobstructed view of the Capitol. On this narrow rectangular tract is an array of storytelling features. Among them are the decade-by-decade Pathway of History, the Court of Three Stars honoring Tennessee musical legends, a powerful World War II memorial, a two-thousand-seat amphitheater popular for weddings, and a ninety-five-bell carillon. Listen for the chiming notes of "Tennessee Waltz." Because this is a state park, there are park rangers who lead informative walks in warm-weather months. The Nashville Farmers' Market is adjacent for picnic goodies.

600 James Robertson Pkwy.
615-741-5280
tnstateparks.com/parks/about/bicentennial-mall

GET SOAKED
AT THE BICENTENNIAL MALL

Watauga, Pigeon, Holston, and Hiwassee. Harpeth, Cumberland, Caney Fork, and Elk. Forked Deer, Obion, Hatchie, and Wolf. People who know Tennessee's waterways recognize those names as rivers in the eastern, middle, and western portions of the state. They are among thirty-one rivers in the Rivers of Tennessee Fountains, each with its own fountainhead, and the cool thing about this feature of Bicentennial Capitol Mall State Park is that the fountains create a splash park where you, your children, or your grandchildren can frolic on one of Nashville's outrageously hot summer days. To dry off, just step over to a two-hundred-foot-long granite map of Tennessee. By the time you walk from Mountain City to Nashville, you'll probably be dry—and you'll likely be ready for another splash in the fountains after continuing on to Memphis.

600 James Robertson Pkwy.
615-741-5280
tnstateparks.com/parks/about/bicentennial-mall

CLIMB THE STONE STEPS
AT PERCY WARNER PARK

Most Nashvillians don't know where the Allée is, but they definitely know where the massive stone staircase that leads into Percy Warner Park is at the end of mansion-lined Belle Meade Boulevard. The Allée is the formal name for the staircase built during the Great Depression, and it is one of several gateways into the 3,180 acres of Percy Warner Park and companion Edwin Warner Park. Together, they are one of the biggest municipal park properties in the nation. After huffing to the top of the Allée, you can enjoy a moderately exertive 2.5-mile hike on the Warner Woods Trail. Elsewhere, the parks offer more trails, equestrian paths, picnic areas, a great nature center, one-way driving routes, a golf course, and other ways to enjoy Mother Nature.

End of Belle Meade Blvd.
615-352-6299
nashville-gov/parks-and-recreation/parks/warner-parks.aspx

WALK ON WATER,
PART I

OK, it's really walk *over* water, but it's still pretty neat that there's a bridge over the Cumberland River just for pedestrians and bicyclists that links Nashville's central business district and tourist zone with the Nissan Stadium side of the Cumberland River. Stroll across the 3,150-foot-long span, built for vehicular traffic from 1907 to 1909, and enjoy the spectacular views of downtown and perhaps look down on a towboat's string of barges or the General Jackson showboat. You might also be a casual witness at someone's wedding. The bridge, one of the longest pedestrian bridges in the world, is named for journalist and civil rights advocate John Seigenthaler, who in the 1950s prevented a suicide attempt by a man who tried to jump into the river. The bridge, which was closed to vehicular traffic in 1998, is on the National Register of Historic Places.

nashvilledowntown.com/go/shelby-street-pedestrian-bridge

WALK ON WATER,
PART II

In the Donelson area is another Cumberland River pedestrian and bicycle bridge, this one of modern construction. The 745-foot-long span means you can walk or bike for thirteen miles from downtown to Percy Priest Dam. It's much narrower than the Seigenthaler Bridge but no less impressive. It comes off a limestone bluff on the east side of the river that's considerably higher than the west side. The solution? Build a massive earthen mound so walkers and bicyclists can spiral back down to the natural elevation. Two Rivers Park and the Wave Country water attraction are at the east side, and you are at the tip of 1,200 acres of urban nature in the Shelby Bottoms Natural Area and Shelby Park when you descend the mound on the west side. The bridge is just downriver from where the much-loved Opryland theme park once drew millions of visitors. You can rent a bike near the bridge from Bike the Greenway.

615-862-8400
greenwaysfornashville.org

615-920-1388
bikethegreenway.net

BOWL
AT PINEWOOD SOCIAL OR DONELSON BOWL

Sometimes it just does your psyche well to take a heavy object and whack something—especially if an adult beverage is available. We're talking bowling here, and there are two very different places to let out some aggression or, looking at it another way, test your athleticism. Pinewood Social in the Rolling Mill Hill development is a hipster place known for its six reclaimed bowling lanes, plus a nice restaurant, coffee lounge, and bocce ball court. Donelson Bowl, by contrast, is so retro that it's hip now, too. It opened in 1960 and bills itself as Nashville's oldest bowling alley. It has twenty-four lanes, cold beer, and a staff that's universally lauded for friendliness. Go knock something down!

Pinewood Social
33 Peabody St.
615-751-8111
pinewoodsocial.com

Donelson Bowl
117 Donelson Pike
615-883-3313
facebook.com/pg/bowl.in-donelson

GAZE INTO THE HEAVENS
AT A STAR PARTY

You've never been to a star party and don't know what one is? Well, you're not alone. Star parties are public events where amateur astronomers set up telescopes and show anyone who is interested what's so intriguing in the night sky. The Barnard-Seyfert Astronomical Society (named for two serious astronomers with ties to Nashville) organizes the monthly events in locations such as the Warner Parks, Long Hunter State Park, and Bells Bend Park, places with as little light pollution as possible. They are your chance to see the rings of Saturn, the moons of Jupiter, the great spot of Jupiter, and even sights beyond the solar system. Peering into a telescope is oh so different from seeing pictures in an astronomy book. You're also welcome at the society's indoor meetings if the astronomy bug bites you.

Various outdoor locations
bsasnashville.com

CULTURE AND HISTORY

LEARN HISTORY, LOVE MUSIC
AT THE RYMAN AUDITORIUM

You say the Ryman Auditorium looks more like a church than one of the world's most loved concert venues? You're right, because it opened its doors in 1892 as the Union Gospel Tabernacle, an ecumenical church inspired by the powerful preaching of evangelist Sam Jones and largely funded by a riverboat captain named Tom Ryman. Jones preached Ryman's funeral and proposed changing the name to the Ryman Auditorium, and the red brick building became the location for appearances by everyone from Teddy Roosevelt, Enrico Caruso, Sarah Bernhardt, and George Washington Carver to the Metropolitan Opera, W. C. Fields, Katharine Hepburn, and Bob Hope. Learn the story of promoter Lula C. Naff, who kept the building vibrant for decades and made it the full-time residence of the Grand Ole Opry from 1943 to 1974.

116 Fifth Ave. N.
615-889-3060
ryman.com

TIP

The Ryman's history lesson is great, but go for some music. The theater returned from the dead in 1994 after a multimillion-dollar project that preserved its extraordinary acoustics and original pews. It's fine to bring a seat cushion. While The Grand Ole Opry is here for winter shows, artists of many genres fill other dates. Think Neil Diamond, Ringo Starr, Kesha, Garth Brooks, and the Foo Fighters, among many others.

WELL, OUR PARTHENON HAS A ROOF

Tell your globetrotting friends they can save themselves a trip to Greece because they can see what the Parthenon originally looked like by visiting Centennial Park. Yep, that's a full-scale replica of the Athenian temple at Centennial Park in midtown Nashville, and ours has a roof that protects a forty-two-foot-tall statue of Athena. A six-foot-tall statue of Mercury stands on her outstretched palm. The building exists as a second-generation leftover from the Tennessee Centennial Exposition in 1897. The Parthenon built for the exposition was made of plaster and lathe and gradually deteriorated, but the city loved it and built the current concrete structure in 1925. To see a towering rendering of the 1897 event and other historic Nashville scenes, check out the murals inside the Gaylord Opryland Resort (page 61).

2500 West End Ave.
615-862-8431
conservancyonline.com

MIX OLD WITH NEW
AT BELLE MEADE PLANTATION

Touring an authentic Southern plantation is one thing, but it's something else entirely to zip around the grounds on a Segway, enjoy a good Chardonnay, or play some bocce ball after touring this antebellum home. Belle Meade Plantation, which has been attracting people since 1820, thereby claiming to be Nashville's original tourist attraction, adds contemporary leisure activities to historical interpretation. Belle Meade's history is rich indeed—it once was among America's top Thoroughbred racehorse breeding farms, and five U.S. presidents have visited it—but its history is only the start. There's a nice restaurant, the plantation's own winery offers wine pairing programs, bourbon is in the picture again, and you can dust off your croquet game if you wish. See, there's much to do after peering into history inside the mansion itself.

110 Leake Ave.
615-356-0501
bellemeadeplantation.com

QUICK, GET TO THE FRIST
BEFORE THINGS CHANGE

The Frist Art Museum is not like most museums you have visited. It has no permanent collection. Instead, it is a venue for an ever-changing series of exhibitions and special events that spotlight art from around the world in an imposing, historic art deco building that once was Nashville's main post office. Exhibitions about American art from World War I, images from Nashville's civil rights struggle, or contemporary Asian art are interspersed with artifacts from ancient Egypt, Parisian fashion, or iconic European sports cars. Highly popular is the Martin ArtQuest Gallery, with interactive stations, where you can make a print, paint a watercolor, or create a sculpture. This gallery is included in adult admission and is free to anyone eighteen and younger.

919 Broadway
615-244-3340
fristartmuseum.org

TIPS

The Frist is open until 9 p.m. Thursday and Friday evenings, when college students are admitted free of charge (with college ID), and visitors are likely to find in-gallery activities, a film, or free music in the Frist Café.

The Frist's gift shop is well known as *the* place for truly artful gifts. Find prints, books, blown glass, jewelry, and other creations of local and regional artisans.

DISCOVER ART
AT FISK UNIVERSITY

If ever a city had an underappreciated treasure, it is Nashville's Carl Van Vechten Gallery at Fisk University. The gallery occupies a building completed in 1889 as the first gymnasium at any predominantly black college in America. Any hint of its athletic past is long gone, replaced by extraordinary artwork, mostly from an array of African-American and African artists. The gallery owns four thousand pieces, so only a small percentage is shown at any one time. Among its holdings is the 101-piece Stieglitz Collection of Modern Art (Picasso, Cézanne, Renoir, and more), a gift from Stieglitz's widow, artist Georgia O'Keeffe. Fisk and the Crystal Bridges Museum in Bentonville, Arkansas, share ownership of the Stieglitz Collection, which rotates between them every two years.

1000 Seventeenth Ave. N.
615-329-8720
fisk.edu/galleries/the-carl-van-vechten-gallery

TIP

Slip next door to Cravath Hall and climb the stairs to the second floor to admire a set of murals by Aaron Douglas, a key artist of the Harlem Renaissance and the founding chair of Fisk's art department. Jubilee Hall is another Fisk jewel.

LEARN ABOUT A COMPLEX MAN
AT THE HERMITAGE

Andrew Jackson was a lightning rod throughout his tumultuous years on earth and remains so today. Learning about him is the reason to visit The Hermitage, his retreat and refuge that many historians call the best-preserved early presidential home. Jackson, of course, was the seventh U.S. president, a populist from the frontier instead of an aristocrat from the East. He also was a judge, a military hero, a slave owner, and the force behind the infamous Trail of Tears. The Hermitage tells his story well and unflinchingly. Docents guide you through the home, and there's an audio tour of the gardens, grounds, and the tomb where Jackson and his beloved wife, Rachel, are buried.

4580 Rachel's Ln.
615-889-2941
thehermitage.com

GET AN AUTOGRAPH
AT THE SOUTHERN FESTIVAL OF BOOKS

Legislative Plaza is so much more fun during the Southern Festival of Books than when the Legislature is in session. People are happy, discussions are about books instead of legislation, and approximately two hundred authors from all genres are present for readings, panel discussions, and book signings. The three-day bibliophile extravaganza is a freebie and even includes a bit of music. This *is* Nashville, after all. It's all a project of Humanities Tennessee, a nonprofit that promotes lifelong learning and civil discourse, quite a nice goal in these argumentative times. If you're feeling benevolent, you can dine with an author in the grandeur of the War Memorial Auditorium at the fundraising Authors in the Round Dinner and get that author's book to take home.

Legislative Plaza
Sixth Ave. N. between Charlotte Ave. and Union St.
615-770-0006
humanitiestennessee.org/content/what-we-do

ROCK IT
AT WAR MEMORIAL AUDITORIUM

When the Grand Ole Opry went on the air in 1925, something even grander happened—the completion of the magnificent War Memorial Building, honoring all Tennesseans who served in World War I and naming the 3,400 casualties. A century later, both are going strong. Doric columns lead to a heroic statue called Victory and a 1,661-seat auditorium with near-perfect acoustics. The Nashville Symphony performed here for five decades, as did the Opry from 1939 to 1943, adding Bill Monroe, Ernest Tubb, and Minnie Pearl to its cast. The mind-boggling list of individuals who have spoken or performed here includes Martin Luther King Jr., Bette Davis, Bette Midler, Barry Manilow, Kiss, Jim Croce, Frank Zappa, Lou Reed, Jack White, R.E.M., Paramore, and Mumford & Sons. Although its next-door neighbor is the state Capitol, the venue seems hidden to many. It shouldn't be, because as its management says, "War Memorial Auditorium Rocks!"

301 Sixth Ave. N.
615-782-4030
wmarocks.com

TIP

Check out *The Attic Sessions* series on the auditorium's website. These are short documentary films featuring emerging artists and touring musicians recorded at the auditorium and showcasing new generations of talent.

SHARPEN YOUR ARTISTIC EYE
AT FIRST SATURDAY ART CRAWL

First Saturday Art Crawl Downtown lets you visit a slew of art galleries and unashamedly say, "I'm just looking." More than two dozen diverse galleries and non-traditional gallery spaces open from 6 to 9 p.m. the first Saturday of every month, so you can sashay through a compact downtown district, sip wine, and recall some facts from your long-ago art history course. Each month, about two thousand people nod appreciatively as they stroll from Hatch Show Print's Haley Gallery (page 122) up to the Fifth Avenue of the Arts and its collection of galleries near Union Street, detour to spaces inside the Arcade, and perhaps stray to the 21c Museum Hotel. If this gallery space were under one roof, it would surpass the twenty-five thousand square feet at the Frist Art Museum (page 90).

Along 5th Ave. and beyond
615-254-2040
nashvilledowntown.com/events/first-saturday-art-crawl

TIPS

A smaller art crawl called Arts & Music at Wedgewood-Houston happens the same night as the downtown soiree in the evolving WeHo neighborhood. For details: am-wh.com

The North Nashville art scene bustles the fourth Saturday of every month during the Jefferson Street Art Crawl. For details: facebook.com/JSACTN

HIKE THROUGH HISTORY
AT FORT NEGLEY

Every day, tens of thousands of people on I-65 zoom past the largest inland fort built during the Civil War and never think of stopping. You shouldn't be one of them. Fort Negley tells multiple stories about the Civil War while you walk casually through the massive structure. The Confederacy surrendered Nashville early in the war, and the Union immediately began work to make it the most fortified city in the nation except for Washington, D.C., itself. More than 2,700 laborers (mainly runaway slaves and free blacks) did the work. Between six hundred and eight hundred died, and only 310 received pay. The fort deteriorated as the decades wore on, the Civilian Conservation Corps did restoration work on it during the Depression, and it is now is a Nashville park. This piece of American history awaits your exploration.

1100 Fort Negley Blvd.
615-862-8470
nashville.gov/parks-and-recreation/historic-sites/fort-negley

CREATE YOUR OWN EXPLANATION
OF *GHOST BALLET*

Ghost Ballet for the East Bank Machineworks is the title of the attention-getting sculpture on the other side of the Cumberland River from Lower Broadway—the one many people think is an homage to roller coasters. It's not. The artist had other things in mind, as did creators of more than fifty pieces of public art all over the city. Some are super-realistic, such as the naked (and we mean really naked) fifteen-foot-tall dancers in *Musica* at Music Row; some are humorous, such as *Handlebar Moustache* in East Nashville; and some are sobering and thought-provoking, such as *Witness Walls* at Public Square Park. Be observant—they're everywhere.

Almost everywhere you look
nashville.gov/arts-commission/experience-art

TIP
The Metro Arts Commission outlines a five-mile art bike tour at the website above, and explorenashvilleart.com showcases many more art destinations that are visible but are privately owned. An example: Chet Atkins awaits you at Fifth Avenue North and Union Street.

MARVEL
AT AN EGYPTIAN-MOTIF PRESBYTERIAN CHURCH

74

Egyptian Revival, an architectural style inspired by Napoleon's conquest of Egypt, reached Nashville in 1851 with the third incarnation of Downtown Presbyterian Church. Famous Philadelphia architect William Strickland designed it while overseeing another project in town, the state Capitol. Inside and out are remarkable reminders of ancient Egypt, which have nothing to do with Presbyterianism. Perhaps even more impressive is the church's 2,709-pipe organ. Guests are welcome to walk through 9 a.m. to 3 p.m. weekdays, and guided tours for five people or more are available (call ahead). Of course, showing up on Sunday morning guarantees you hear that magnificent organ. You may even be able to tour *inside* the organ. The congregation dates to 1814 (Presidents Jackson and Polk were worshipers), and it is a mainstay in ministry to the homeless and urban poor. Consider volunteering Saturday mornings to help serve a community breakfast.

154 Fifth Ave. N.
615-254-7584
dpchurch.com

102

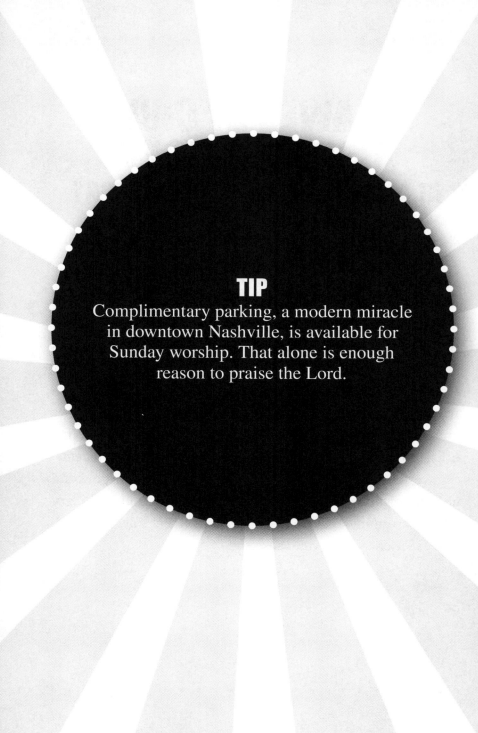

TIP

Complimentary parking, a modern miracle in downtown Nashville, is available for Sunday worship. That alone is enough reason to praise the Lord.

BE AWED BY CIVIL RIGHTS HISTORY
AT THE NASHVILLE PUBLIC LIBRARY

Nashville didn't escape the civil rights turmoil of the 1950s and 1960s, but it did avoid much of the violence visited on other cities nationwide. A major reason was exacting preparation for well-orchestrated, peaceful protests that emanated from four predominantly black colleges and universities—American Baptist, Fisk, Meharry, and Tennessee A&I. That story is told in emotional detail in the Civil Rights Room of the Nashville Public Library. The room overlooks Church Street and Seventh Avenue North, a focal point for segregated lunch counter protests. The room's centerpiece is a circular table resembling a lunch counter. Perch on the stools and read about students' resolve to end injustice, and then examine fourteen powerful newspaper photos from the era, especially ones showing angry adults screaming at little first-graders on their way to school. The experience gives you pause.

615 Church St.
615-862-5800
library.nashville.org/research/collection/civil-rights-room

TIP

History collides with contemporary dining at Woolworth on 5th, a restaurant/lounge/music venue that replicates the look and feel of the Woolworth department store that once occupied the same location. Everyone is welcome at this lunch counter. For details: woolworthonfifth.com

MEET NATURE AND ART
AT CHEEKWOOD

Who would want to visit some old mansion built in 1929 by some old rich dude? You would, if you have half a brain. Cheekwood Estate & Gardens transcends most people's expectations of a tour of a historic home. The home, built with money from a grocery empire and Maxwell House Coffee (you know, "good to the last drop"), is a Nashville gem. This thirty-thousand-square-foot, thirty-six-room Georgian structure now houses an impressive art collection, mostly American works from 1910 to 1970, but the natural beauty of the fifty-five-acre estate is usually is what people remember most. The gardens explode every spring with 150,000 bulbs; Thursday nights in summer bustle with entertainment, children's activities, food trucks, and cash bars; autumn is aglow with five thousand chrysanthemums; and Christmas amazes with one million glowing lights throughout the grounds. There's nothing staid about this place.

1200 Forrest Park Dr.
615-356-8000
cheekwood.org

CRANE YOUR NECK AT TWO CLASSIC HOTELS
WHERE THE ATTRACTIONS ARE OVERHEAD

In a world of minimalist hotels accented with chrome and glass, take a trip to another era at the Union Station Hotel and the Hermitage Hotel. In both, the lobby ceilings command your attention. The castle-like Union Station Hotel opened in 1900 to serve passengers on eight railroad lines, and its sixty-five-foot-high barrel-vaulted ceiling accented with Tiffany-style stained glass marked it as a grand structure, indeed. Ten years later, the Beaux-Arts-style Hermitage Hotel opened a few blocks away, and its soaring lobby pulled guests' eyes overhead to admire a ceiling of intricate ornamental plaster and painted glass. Over the decades, both hotels have had their ups and downs, but they have been at the top of the hotel game for years. Step inside, and we guarantee you'll look up. (For more about the Hermitage Hotel, see pages 2 and 10.)

231 Sixth Ave. N.
615-244-3121
thehermitagehotel.com

1001 Broadway
615-726-1001
unionstationhotelnashville.com

WHISTLE PAST THE GRAVEYARD

AT THE NASHVILLE CITY CEMETERY

There's really no reason for the false bravado of whistling past the graveyard at this historic cemetery. It's a beautiful place to tour—it's even a forty-species arboretum—and its headstones offer clues to great stories. Burials began in 1820, and among cemetery celebrities are Charlotte and James Robertson, two of Nashville's founding settlers in 1779, memorialized elsewhere in town on street signs for Charlotte Pike and James Robertson Parkway. Another cemetery resident is William Driver, a sea captain who ended up in landlocked Nashville. Seafaring exploits aside, Driver is why we call the American flag "Old Glory." Driver hid his ship's flag, "Old Glory," from occupying Confederates in the Civil War. To see it now, you have to visit the Smithsonian Institution in Washington, D.C.

1001 Fourth Ave. S.
thenashvillecitycemetery.org
615-862-7970

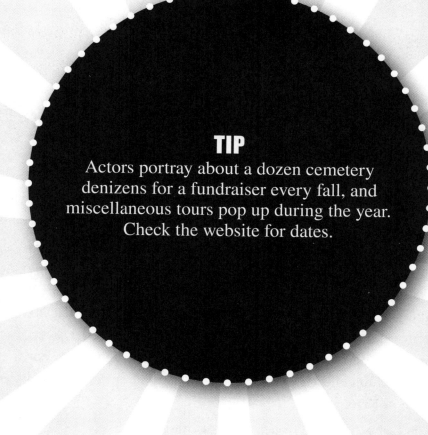

TIP
Actors portray about a dozen cemetery denizens for a fundraiser every fall, and miscellaneous tours pop up during the year. Check the website for dates.

UNEARTH TENNESSEE'S TREASURES
AT THE STATE MUSEUM

For almost forty years, the Tennessee State Museum was practically hidden in the subterranean levels of a state office building. While that museum actually was quite good, it certainly had no street appeal. That changed in 2018, and the formerly buried treasures of the Volunteer State now are extraordinarily visible in a single-purpose, multistory, $160 million structure just north of the state Capitol, Bicentennial Mall, and the Nashville Farmers' Market. The museum offers several permanent exhibits and a full calendar of special displays and events. This is the place to see ten-thousand-year-old mastodon bones, President Andrew Johnson's own ticket to his impeachment trial, banners from the 1920 women's suffrage campaign, and even a jacket and skirt donated by entertainer Tina Turner. Tennessee has managed to collect a passel of interesting stuff since statehood came in 1796.

1000 Rosa L. Parks Blvd.
615-741-2692
tnmuseum.org

GO HIGH-OCTANE
AT LANE MOTOR MUSEUM

You say car museums don't interest you? You'll rethink that after seeing Lane Motor Museum's peculiar collection. Consider the 1964 Peel from the Isle of Man, the world's smallest production car (it's shorter than Brenda Lee is tall); the 1932 Helicron, a propeller-driven beauty Jay Leno drove when he visited; and the 1942 Tatra, a car on skis the Germans wanted to use to cross the Russian steppes. Most of the cars are from outside the United States, meaning you may have never have heard of them. The museum displays about 150 of its more than 530 vehicles, almost all of which run. While you can't touch them, you can walk around them and admire from every angle. One treasure is museum owner Jeff Lane's 1955 MG TF-1500. He began restoring it at age twelve and took the test drive for his driver's license in it.

702 Murfreesboro Pike
615-742-7445
lanemotormuseum.org

TIP
Ask about "basement tours" that provide access to many of the museum's vehicles not currently on display and about the fall fundraiser that includes the opportunity to get behind the wheel of some interesting vehicles.

FEEL REGAL
AT THE SCHERMERHORN SYMPHONY CENTER

If Nashville had real royalty instead of country music royalty, their palace would probably would look like the Schermerhorn Symphony Center. This $123.5 million neoclassical beauty opened in 2006 as home to the Nashville Symphony, one of America's most active recording orchestras and winner of more than a dozen Grammy Awards. Its 1,800-seat Laura Turner Concert Hall has a mechanical system able to flip from concert seating to a ballroom configuration in less than two hours, and hearing its 3,500-pipe concert organ is a pure joy. As palatial as it is, it is not intimidating. People who have never attended a classical concert have enjoyed special nights when performers such as Sheryl Crow, Tony Bennett, Diana Ross, Willie Nelson, Alabama, and Boyz II Men have appeared — in joint performance with the Nashville Symphony.

1 Symphony Pl.
615-687-6400
nashvillesymphony.org

TIP

There are no regular tours of the symphony center, but there are two ways to get a special tour. One is to donate one hundred dollars to the symphony's annual fund, and the other is to gather from twelve to seventy-five people and buy group tickets to a Nashville Symphony performance.

EXPLORE NASHVILLE'S AUTOMOTIVE PAST
AT MARATHON VILLAGE

In the early 1900s, many cities had the potential to become the automotive nexus that Detroit became, even Nashville. Marathon Motor Works, just blocks from Tennessee's Capitol, built a variety of automobiles from 1910 to 1914. Examples of those classic cars are on display in a modest museum in one corner of the former industrial complex, while most of the sprawling facility now constitutes Marathon Village. Marathon Village retains its industrial look and houses shops (including Antique Archaeology, a Jack Daniel's store, and a Harley-Davidson store), work studios, a winery, a distillery, a deli, a coffee house, and more. Learn some history, find a Nashville souvenir, and even bend an elbow at a bar. Friday is food truck day.

1305 Clinton St.
615-327-1010
marathonvillage.net

SPEND A NIGHT WITH THE BARD OF AVON
AT SHAKESPEARE IN THE PARK

Don't let a few chigger bites keep you from meeting Julius Caesar, King Lear, Falstaff, Nick Bottom, or Othello, something you can do stretched out on a blanket or in your own lawn chair at Shakespeare in the Park, a late-summer event in Centennial Park. The Nashville Shakespeare Festival has presented these family-friendly professional productions since 1988. Admission is free, but the NSF must raise $250,000 a year to make the summer shows work. (Actors smile upon a ten-dollar donation, but remember that generosity is a virtue.) The NSF offers a winter production, too, blessedly indoors. Like ol' Will in his day, NSF artistic director Denice Hicks is a local legend, so seeing one of her productions is oh-so-Nashville.

2500 West End Ave.
615-255-2273
nashvilleshakes.org

CONTEMPLATE
AMERICA'S WORST TRAIN WRECK

If not for a marker along the Richland Creek Greenway, you'd likely never know that the worst train wreck in American history happened in Nashville. In 1918, the site was a cornfield. Today, it's a place where walkers, joggers, bicyclists, and moms with kids in strollers pass by in between a Publix supermarket and the Lions Head Shopping Center. Human error put two passenger trains on a collision course at Dutchman's Curve, one traveling at 50 mph and the other at 60 mph. The crash, which killed at least 101 and injured at least 171, was heard two miles away. More than fifty thousand people came to help, search for survivors, or simply see the scene of a tragedy. Reading the marker gives you plenty to contemplate as you traverse the 4.8 miles of this quiet and peaceful greenway.

4601 Murphy Rd.
greenwaysfornashville.org

SEE WHERE LEGISLATIVE SAUSAGE IS MADE

Putting all political sarcasm aside, Tennessee's Capitol is a beautiful building worth visiting. William Strickland, an architectural and engineering rock star of his time and a leader in Greek Revival design, designed the statehouse, which was finished in 1859. (Tour trivia: Strickland died during construction and is buried in the north facade.) Part of his inspiration was the Monument of Lysicrates from 334 BC Athens. When Union troops occupied Nashville early in the Civil War, the Capitol became Fortress Andrew Johnson, but its cannon never were fired in anger. The Tennessee State Museum offers guided tours six times a day.

Charlotte Ave. between Sixth Ave. and Seventh Ave. N.
615-741-0830
tnmuseum.org/exhibits/Tennessee_state_capitol

TIP
Downtown Presbyterian Church at 154 Fifth Ave. N. is another building Strickland designed (page 102). It's the only church with an Egyptian motif you're ever likely to see.

SHOPPING AND FASHION

DO SOME PICKIN'
AT CARTER VINTAGE GUITARS

The Lovin' Spoonful's song says there are "thirteen hundred and fifty-two guitar pickers in Nashville," and all of them probably have been to Carter Vintage Guitars to ogle, pick, or maybe buy one of the 1,200 instruments and amps on display every day. You should go, too, whether or not you're a picker. The display of guitars is artful, and it's a joy to listen to serious musicians try out guitars that interest them. It's quite likely you'll hear a talented session musician or even an A-list entertainer play. The store, which sells about two thousand instruments a year, is easy to find. Just look for the giant Les Paul Gibson guitar mural on Eighth Avenue South next door to the Jackalope Brewing Company.

625 Eighth Ave. S.
615-915-1851
cartervintage.com

TIP

Other stops on a Nashville guitar quest
should include these two gems:

Cotten Music Center

434 Houston St.
615-383-8947
cottenmusic.com

Gruhn Guitars

2120 Eighth Ave. S.
615-256-2033
guitars.com

BUY A POSTER
AT HATCH SHOW PRINT

Nashville's quintessential souvenir is a print from Hatch Show Print, an only-one-in-the-world shop that's been creating entertainment industry art since 1879. Artists using flat-bed presses, hand-carved blocks, and classic lettering staff the shop, now part of the Country Music Hall of Fame and Museum. Hatch thrives because it created a distinctive style and because it didn't abandon eighteenth-century technology. Retro is good at Hatch. The Hatch look that worked for traveling circuses, Roy Acuff, Hank Williams, and Elvis Presley works today for Bonnie Raitt, Chick Corea, Pearl Jam, Diana Ross, and artists of all genres who appear at the nearby Ryman Auditorium; look for the Hatch display there. The shop features a gallery of classic posters and modern takes on the Hatch look, plus guided tours. A lucky few get into a once-a-month printmaking class.

224 Fifth Ave. S.
615-256-2805
hatchshowprint.com

EXPLORE
THE NASHVILLE ARCADE

Nashville's first shopping mall—and one of America's oldest—hides in plain sight between Fourth and Fifth Avenues North. It is the Nashville Arcade, built in 1902. The grand opening in 1903 drew forty thousand people when Nashville's total population was 125,000. Activity isn't that chaotic now in this collection of almost fifty restaurants (a meat-and-three, Mexican, sushi, specialty hot dogs, barbecue, even Ethiopian), shops, offices, and art galleries. The ground level is heavily restaurants and shops, and the mezzanine level is mostly galleries. Overhead is a gabled glass roof, adding to the European flair, which makes sense because the developers' inspiration was the Galleria Vittorio Emanuele II arcade in Milan. The Arcade is most vibrant middays during the week when it bustles with downtown workers and smart kids from nearby Hume-Fogg Academic Magnet High School, one of the nation's best prep schools.

65 Arcade Alley
615-248-6673
thenashvillearcade.com

GO NUTS
AT THE PEANUT SHOP

The Nashville Arcade creates a gentle wind tunnel dispersing the aroma of roasting peanuts that practically pulls you inside the Peanut Shop, a tiny retail space that has been a hit since 1927. Little Bertha, the peanut roasting machine, is at it again. The friendliness of the owners (two effervescent sisters) is equally intoxicating, and it's easy to keep saying, "I'll have a quarter-pound of those chocolate-covered almonds, too. And maybe some of those Spanish reds." This is definitely old-school retailing. Bins of peanuts, cashews, almonds, and other treats fill glass-fronted cases, and your orders are scooped out and weighed on the shop's original countertop scales. You can satisfy your craving for more with an online purchase, just as fans from as far away as Australia and England do.

19 Arcade
615-256-3394
nashvillenut.com

SHOP, DINE, AND STROLL
THROUGH 12SOUTH

12South is a bustling, multiblock stretch of Twelfth Avenue South where long-time Nashvillians say, "Why didn't I buy one of those distressed buildings twenty years ago?" Upscale restaurants, casual eateries, craft beer places, a local pizza parlor, coffee dispensaries, hair salons, and trendy boutiques, including one owned by Nashville native-turned-actress Reese Witherspoon fill this walkable district south of Belmont University. Building murals add extra color, and it's practically a law to take your photo with the *I Believe in Nashville* painting. A Christian bookstore, the Islamic Center of Nashville, and a pawnshop preceded gentrification and add their own flavors. Speaking of flavors, Las Paletas at the neighborhood's far south end sells healthy-sounding Mexican ice pops made with fresh fruits, veggies, and nuts.

visitmusiccity.com/visitors/neighborhoods/12south

TIP
Defy your cardiologist and enjoy a Tuck Special at Edley's Bar-B-Que. That's beef brisket, spicy pimento cheese, a fried egg, and two sauces on a soft bun. You can almost hear the little arteries popping shut. For details: edleysbbq.com

FIND ONE MAN'S TRASH, ETC.,
AT THE NASHVILLE FLEA MARKET

Flea markets are a huge industry (1,100 locations in the United States and a total sales volume of $30 billion), so noting that the Nashville Flea Market is considered one of the top ten in the nation says some prowling around here is the thing to do. It happens the fourth weekend of every month at the Nashville Fairgrounds (the third weekend in December, of course) with between eight hundred and 1,200 dealers and vendors in an average of two thousand booths. Put on some comfortable shoes, sharpen your negotiating skills, and expect to find practically anything under the sun.

625 Smith Ave.
615-862-5016
thefairgrounds.com/fleamarket

GET MUSICAL
AT GRIMEY'S

Make sure you have some mad money when you walk into Grimey's New and Preloved Music and Books because you're almost certain to find an impulse purchase among the vinyl, CDs, books, T-shirts, and postcards that fill the store. Grimey's and the companion Grimey's Too were sibling institutions on Eighth Avenue South for years and now are combined in a bigger space in East Nashville. Much emphasis is put on new and independent acts in all genres, but you can go nuts finding classics from Miles Davis and Duke Ellington, Webb Wilder and Duane Eddy, Kiss, and Carole King. There are many "Eureka!" moments as you flip through bins of albums and search bookshelves for treasures. Follow Grimey's on Twitter for frequent artist appearances that can pop up with little notice. It's a Nashville thing.

1060 East Trinity Ln.
615-254-4801
grimeys.com

TIP
There's a 10 percent discount on everything preloved on Mondays.

WALTZ ACROSS TEXAS
WITH E.T.

True country music fans know "E.T." means Hall of Famer Ernest Tubb, not some space critter. Take a selfie with the Texas Troubadour's towering bronze statue inside the Ernest Tubb Record Shop on Lower Broadway. It's a downtown fixture as much as the honky tonks. You can almost can hear E.T.'s gravelly voice singing "Waltz Across Texas" as you poke through the record bins and admire scores of publicity photos and paintings of country stars adorning the walls. You'll find classic albums, CDs, box sets, and more. If you're lucky, you'll chance into a presentation of the Ernest Tubb Midnite Jamboree. This post-Opry show (second in broadcast longevity only to the Opry itself) is usually at the Texas Troubadour Theatre near the Opry House, but in-store special broadcasts do happen — just like the old days.

417 Broadway
615-255-7503
etrecordshop.com

GO ANTIQUING
ON EIGHTH AVENUE SOUTH

Want an antique brass chandelier? How about a sailboat rudder? Or perhaps a Polaroid Swinger camera, a railroad lantern, or a Nashville Junior League cookbook from 1964? Just prowl Eighth Avenue South, an elongated treasure trove of old stuff. Start almost in The Gulch at the Downtown Antique Mall and work your way south to a cluster of other malls and stand-alone stores near the intersection with Wedgewood Avenue. Just off Eighth on Wedgewood is yet another big mall, the Tennessee Antique Mall. Ease into any of them, and you may not emerge for hours as you poke through multiple sellers' antiques, collectibles, decorative items, and, well, just stuff. You'll find true antiques, reproductions, and items identical to things you threw away years ago. Today, someone will pay good money for the Lassie lunchbox you tossed out.

Downtown Antique Mall
612 Eighth Ave. S.
615-256-6616

Tennessee Antique Mall
654 Wedgewood Ave.
615-259-4077

BE A PICKER
AT ANTIQUE ARCHAEOLOGY

Mike Wolfe is watched and admired by millions of viewers of the History Channel's *American Pickers*. Finder of old stuff. Keeper of history. Protector of the past. Teller of tales. That's why so many people make a pilgrimage to Antique Archaeology, his seemingly cluttered (but quite in character) store in a once-abandoned industrial building that only in recent years did many Nashvillians know housed an automobile factory from the early 1900s.Visitors/shoppers come to inspect old Coca-Cola machines, rusted bicycles, ancient portrait photos of unnamed people, and other examples of the past's flotsam and jetsam. It's more than a trip down Memory Lane. It's really time travel.

1300 Clinton St.
615-810-9906
antiquearchaeology.com

GOTTA GET A GOO GOO,
IT'S GOOOOOD

Chocoholics know one of Nashville's great distinctions is that the first combination candy was invented here. It's the world-famous Goo Goo Cluster, and what a combination it is—chocolate, peanuts, caramel, and marshmallow. It rolled out of Standard Candy Co. in 1912 and is doing great in a highly competitive confections industry more than a century later. Goo Goo Clusters were a long-time advertiser on the Grand Ole Opry (page 32), but it's not true that their name is an acronym for the famous radio show. Variations include one with pecans and one with peanut butter, and there has been a Goo Goo ice cream. Learn the whole history, including how they were considered "a nutritious lunch" in the calorie-starved Great Depression, at the Goo Goo Shop, dedicated to all things Goo Goo. Make your own Goo Goo Cluster at a Thursday or Friday chocolate class.

116 Third Ave. S.
615-490-6685
googoo.com

FREE YOUR INNER BIBLIOPHILE
AT PARNASSUS BOOKS

Author Ann Patchett saw Nashville's last independent bookstore and its last major chain bookstore close and knew she had to react. She did by joining with friends Karen Hayes and Mary Grey to open Parnassus Books, a comfortable, warm, and inviting bookstore complete with knowledgeable clerks, children's storytelling time, book signings, and friendly greeter dogs. As she told Stephen Colbert in a *Comedy Central* interview worth finding on YouTube or the store's website, "When there isn't a bookstore in your city, there's an incredible void because what you realize is that the bookstore isn't just the place to buy books. It's a community center. I can't imagine a world without bookstores." Patchett, Hayes, and Grey have given Nashville a stellar community center and many reasons to visit it. Why Parnassus? Mount Parnassus was the home of literature, learning, and music in Greek mythology.

3900 Hillsboro Pike
615-953-2243
parnassusbooks.net

TIPS

For a hard-to-find, out-of-print, used, or rare volume, inquire at Elder's Bookstore. For details: eldersbookstore.com

For more old books, plus vinyl records and musical instruments, head to Rhino Booksellers. For details: rhinobooksnashville.com

BE CRAFTY
AT THE TENNESSEE CRAFT FAIR

If your best craft handiwork was a woven potholder or a plastic lanyard at summer camp, you'll be green with envy at the Tennessee Craft Fair. These are three-day events every May and September when artist-inhabited tents pop up like giant mushrooms on the spacious grounds of Centennial Park. The Parthenon provides a backdrop — and perhaps artistic inspiration. You can buy the works of juried, award-winning artists and crafters who work in clay, textiles, glass, paint, photography, and other media. Don't look for potholders and lanyards. Also in the mix are a special tent for kids' activities, food vendors, and demonstrations of how art objects come to be. Admission to both fairs is free.

Centennial Park
2500 West End Ave.
tennesseecraft.org./events/craft-fairs

TIP
Early every October, Tennessee Craft Week schedules craft events across Tennessee. Find one that will inspire a road trip at tennesseecraft.org/tennessee-craft-week.

LET MANUEL
DRESS YOU UP

You may never drop $600 on a super-fancy western shirt or $2,500 (or more) on a super-super-fancy rhinestone-studded jacket, but internationally famous fashion designer Manuel does have some more modest items to peruse while you admire his blazingly colorful inventory of high-fashion clothing. Manuel, who put Johnny Cash in black, has created clothing for Porter Wagoner, Marty Stuart, George Jones, Jack White, Robert Redford, Miranda Lambert, and scores of other entertainment giants. It's a treat just to think about buying something he created. Everything here is Manuel's design, and a team of six talented needle-and-thread artists sewed them on site.

2804 Columbine Pl.
615-321-5444
manuelcouture.com

EXPERIENCE PEACE, LOVE & ROCK 'N' ROLL
AT TWO OLD HIPPIES

The peace symbol door handle to Two Old Hippies sets the tone for a chilled-out shopping experience in an aging one-story building that once housed a printing business and then a commercial bakery. You'll find rock 'n' roll photos and memorabilia on the walls, a genuine "Magic Bus" (a VW van with a brilliant floral paint job), distinctive apparel for men and women (Woodstock-worthy dresses, vintage leather jackets, wide belts, and much more), tees for kids, books (think Lennon, Jagger, and Kiss), and artisan products in a market area. The two old hippies who opened the boutique in The Gulch in 2011 call it a "hip mini department store of sorts." This is Nashville, so it's no surprise that The Vault features their own Breedlove, Bedell, and Weber acoustical instruments and that there's live music four nights a week. Peace, brother.

401 Twelfth Ave. S.
615-254-7999
twooldhippies.com

I BELIEVE IN NASHVILLE

© 2012   #ibelieveinnashville

SUGGESTED
ITINERARIES

ONLY IN NASHVILLE

Go Grand at the Grand Ole Opry, 32

Learn History, Love Music at the Ryman Auditorium, 86

Clap Loudly at *Music City Roots*, 34

Jump On In with The Time Jumpers, 33

Steep Yourself in Country Music, 42

Well, Our Parthenon Has a Roof, 88

Get the Beat at the Musicians Hall of Fame, 44

Discover Art at Fisk University, 92

Attend a Tomato Party, 28

BUY A TREASURE OR A TREAT

Buy a Poster at Hatch Show Print, 122

Explore Nashville's Automotive Past at Marathon Village, 114

Go Antiquing on Eighth Avenue South, 129

Pack Your Picnic Basket at the Nashville Farmers' Market, 22

Quick, Get to the Frist before Things Change, 90

Go Nuts at the Peanut Shop, 124

Gotta Get a Goo Goo, It's Goooood, 131

CHOW DOWN

RIGHT DOWNTOWN

OUTDOOR FUN

ACTIVITIES
BY SEASON

Nashville is a four-season city, and most of its attractions and activities are available year round. However, festivals, special events, and some specific activities brighten certain seasons. Here's some guidance.

SPRING

Run, Jog, or Trot for 13.1 or 26.2 Miles, 69

Get an Earful at Musicians Corner, 54

Be Crafty at the Tennessee Craft Fair, 134

Watch Bruins and Bisons Battle It Out, 70

Get Dressy at the Iroquois Steeplechase, 75

Roll around Town on a Bicycle, 74

Walk, Eat, Repeat on a Food Tour, 7

SUMMER

Hit a Nashville Sounds Homerun, 64

Take a Lazy Float on the Harpeth River, 73

Join the Sing-Along at CMA Fest, 53

Spend a Night with the Bard of Avon at Shakespeare in the Park, 115

Get Soaked at the Bicentennial Mall, 78

Attend a Tomato Party, 28

Walk on Water, Part I, 80

AUTUMN

WINTER

INDEX

145